A BRIEF HIST[ORY]

Lee Arey, a Port Townsend native and son of one of the [founders of the Beckett] Point Fishermen's Club (BPFC), took time out of a home remodel and reflected over the history of the club. In the war years of the 40's he recalled that when fishing for salmon that "it wasn't unusual to have a limit of six in the boat for each fishermen."

In 1938 Beckett Point was on the county delinquent tax roles.

A close knit group of Quimper Peninsula sportsmen filed articles of incorporation, purchased Beckett Point and founded our community.

No water, no power and no hassles describe those initial years. Rockfish were abundant. Kids fished from small boats anchored in front of small cabins, honing their skills for the big game fish, Salmon. Chinook were fished in April and May, the Kings were in by June and fishing continued for Silvers in July.

On the North side of the point, off Swede Row, there was a large kelp bed. Fishermen kept their larger fishing boats out beyond the sea plants. It was slow going at low tide. Skiffs were barely able to get through the sodden mass of vegetation. The kelp disappeared in the fifties and took the habitat that attracted fish of all types close to shore.

Great fishing and solitude came at a price. Lots first sold for $50! Many families held four or more pieces of property. Resales went as high as $300 several years later.

A marine railroad was built on the north side near the present boat ramp. A gas-powered winch was used to pull boats to a point above the beach where they were stored. The railroad was removed in the late 50's.

In the 50's a spring was developed to feed a system of holding tanks and pumps. Power marched down the hill on new poles that also brought the telephones. With power and water several families moved to the beach and the rest is history. New water systems, paved roads, TV satellites and a host of new members filled out the Point's dance card. Things have never been the same.

Down the hill, onto the point with Discovery Bay and Diamond Point to the West

In 1792 when Captain George Vancouver sailed into what he called the "perfect harbor" he expected Discovery Bay to someday be a world-class port. Instead, the bay became a world class get-away. Located close enough to enjoy historic Port Townsend and far enough away to be a still, calm place with stunning night skies, howling storms and warm summer afternoons, Beckett offers all the good things of the Pacific Northwest. For more than a hundred families, Beckett Point has become a tranquil way of life, a valued tradition and a place that is indeed "A PERFECT HARBOR."

THE EXPLORERS

In 1790 aboard the *Princess Real*, Manuel Quimper who was making an eastward investigation of the Strait of Juan de Fuca discovered a bay now called Dungeness Bay. His ensign was sent in a longboat further eastward where he discovered another bay, named it Puerto de Bodega Y Quadra and a distinctive island at its entrance. He named the island Isla de Carrasco. The Quimper peninsula was so named around 1838 by the U.S. Coast Survey.

In April 1792 British explorer and surveyor, Vancouver, entered the Strait of Juan de Fuca having departed England a year earlier. He had sailed around the Cape of Good Hope, surveyed a portion of the Australian coast, spent time in Tahiti and re-supplied in Hawaii. Having visited the major bays of the coast of what is now Washington, Vancouver was looking for an anchorage where he could refit his ship and rest his crew. He sailed up the strait and found refuge in what he described as one of the finest harbors in the world. He named it Port Discovery after his ship. It is now called Discovery Bay. Many places in the Pacific Northwest were named by him and his crew. It is likely someone named Beckett was part of his crew. A shore station was established near today's Mill Point.

Vancouver's writings include passages stating he could not "believe any uncultivated country had ever been discovered exhibiting so rich a picture." He thus named snow covered Mt. Baker after one of his lieutenants. This land was bountiful with shrubs, berries, flowering plants and towering trees. He refitted Discovery including re-masting, the masts taken from the forest near Adelma Beach. From Port Discovery he began to survey.

In the immediate area from Port Discovery he charted and named Port Townsend and Hood Canal. Vancouver and his botanist, Archibald Menzies visited and named Protection Island, the reason being its location opposite the mouth of Port Discovery and affording protection to that harbor. They noted with novelty the lush vegetation and wildflowers. They also noted vast flights of water fowl. Sometime after, Discovery moved north to the site of Seattle and mapped that part of Puget Sound named after his senior officer. The accompanying Vessel *Chatham* mapped the San Juan Islands.

There isn't a very complete historical account other than seafarers seeking refuge surrounding Discovery until the mid 1850's. The Kiallam or S'Klallam people have occupied this area for millennia with camps and villages on and around Discovery Bay. During BPFC 2007 sanitation project excavation, artifacts were unearthed giving views to the earlier inhabitants that dwelled here.

In 1858 Port Discovery Mill was established on the west shore today known as Mill Point. Another mill was established at the foot of the Bay. Port Discovery was an important coastal port well into the 20th century. Several of today's residents of Beckett Point relate to knowledge that the Mill's labor force encompassed natives encamped at Beckett Point and transported to work across the bay.

With the changes the 20th century brought to the area, Port Townsend became a major port. The military presence at Fort Warden and Fort Flagler encouraged development on the Quimper Peninsula. The post depression era was prime time for the founding of a sportsman's paradise, Cape George Fishermen, Inc.

Entrance to Discovery Bay with Protection Island in the background

ARTICLES OF CORPORATION

In the late 1930's a group of sportsmen met on the shores of what is today Cape George Colony.

The land at Beckett Point was available for purchase. Handshakes were made, purchase agreements were drawn up, and Articles of Corporation were filed July 1, 1939 in the name of Cape George Fishermen's, Inc.

N.W. Raynor, Roy Dale, H.L. Heitzler, Lyall Arey and Cecil Guptill came together for the purpose of forming this corporation. At this time a group of trustees which consisted of N.W. Raynor, Roy Dale, H. L. Heitzler, Lyall Arey, Bert Carr, Bruce Blevins, S.J. Lockhart and Cecil Guptill was established. The corporation was formed for the following purpose:

1) To provide recreational area for members of the corporation.
2) To promote and stimulate interest in salt water fishing and provide for competition.
3) To promote the highest standards of sportsmanship.
4) To assist in the observance and enforcement of our game laws.
5) To purchase, lease from others and to acquire, sell, convey, transfer leases to others and otherwise dispose or encumber resale of personal property. The original Articles of Corporation were set to expire at 50 years. The filing and a recording fee of $25 were completed July 31, 1939. A board of trustees numbering 8 was established. In 1954 this was amended to be 10 in number of which 2 shall be "lady" members.

In the 1980's it was determined that Cape George Fishermen, Inc. did not comply with state law in that a nonprofit corporation's name shall not end with Inc., Company or Corporation. It was then on May 7, 1992 that Cape George Fishermen's Inc. quit claimed Government lots 1, 2, & 3 in section 23, Township 30 N. Range 2 West to Cape George Fishermen's Association. On August 5, 1993 Articles of Amendment were recorded changing name to Beckett Point Fishermen's Club.

BECKETT POINT INFRASTRUCTURE

Beckett Point is located on the northeast portion of Discovery Bay. The point includes a lagoon measuring 6.6 acres which was formerly open to the South. The opening was filled in the 1940's to facilitate road establishment and point development. The tidal opening was near South Beach Annex lot #28 and until being filled access to the South across the opening was via a bridge. In December, 1988 a state hydraulic permit application was approved to perform work on the lagoon. The purpose was to remove logs to the periphery and cover them with dirt and ground cover. The pond consisted mainly of fresh water from area run-off. In the summer the pond regressed to 25% of winter size exposing mud where no growth occurred and stagnant water and pond scum developed. Some of the proposed project was completed and the results deemed successful. The maximum elevation of the spit is 10 feet and all is located in the 100 year coastal flood designation. Currently there are approximately 160 members owning some 85 acres of land, the majority of which are small cottages that serve as weekend or vacation housing. Each lease holding member has an equal voice in the operation of the community. Property values have escalated dramatically in recent years and now many are being converted to full time residences. The city water installation in 1988 and the completion of the onsite enclosed sewage system in 2008 have, and will continue to have, a major influence on the point.

POWER AT BECKETT POINT

Up to 1950 it appears that existing cabins had their own self contained power units. At this time Cape George Fishermen's Inc addressed installation of power. Installation was approved at a fee of $3,900. Money was borrowed with a bank note and guaranteed by the trustees. Cabin hook ups were to be paid for by the leaseholders and payment on the installation was to be repaid by member assessments of $15 per year. As time went on, power was extended through the point with telephone wire being hung on the power poles. Today we have an Internet connection, cable TV and are surely into the 21st century.

WATER AT BECKETT POINT

Along with power arriving, water was close behind. Up to this time, leaseholders were packing in their own water. In 1951 the spring known as Big Spring was rudimentarily developed. Big Spring is a subterranean spring located in the southeast section of Tax Lot #3 at approximately 100 feet of elevation. Water flowed through a catch basin into a (at places open) delivery system, gravity flowed delivery to the cabins and a fire system. Excerpts from the January 18, 1951 Trustees meeting valued the system at $6,381. It appears almost immediately water supply became an issue, as the 1953 minutes stated that water supplies needed to be increased.

In 1956, water shortage was again addressed. Considerable discussion was given to funding new spring development costs by selling a stand of timber on the north property line. It was eventually funded by assessing leaseholders the utility service charge. Our spring system was improved in that water at Big Spring flowed through the catch basin and proceeded 8/10's of a mile to the pump station located adjacent to South Beach Annex Lot #9. A second spring (Little Spring) was put on line, Little Spring being located on the South edge of Tax Lot #2 at a 30 foot elevation. Water flowed through a catch basin to the pump station near Lot #9. The pump station had a 6,650 gallon capacity. The water was then pumped to reservoirs located on the South hillside of Tax Lot #2 at 200 feet elevation. Water was then transferred by gravity feed to the leaseholders.

During 1968 a well drilling company was hired to drill and tap the aquifer beneath Beckett Point. Two 600 foot attempts were made, with unsatisfactory water quality resulting and the well drilling project was halted.

In 1971 a committee was formed to explore expansion of the water system. Jack Meyer was appointed chairman. In August of 1979 a critical water situation arose with water rationing put into effect that summer. A member committee monitored the supply daily and a flag system was put up. The color of the flag displayed let members know our volume of storage at that particular day.

In 1979, exploration for revamping our system was put into effect. A letter was sent to Port Townsend City Engineers stating that Beckett Point would like to participate in the City water expansion project that was currently being undertaken.

In 1982 the club explored obtaining water from Ocean Grove, repairing our own system and installing new tanks. In 1984 the DSHS notified the Club that our water system was inadequate to volume and due to open surface, water contamination health hazards existed. The time had come to upgrade. A deal was made through PUD, bids were let and construction of today's system completed and operational in June 1988 at a cost of $1,788 per tap. It might be noted that remnants of Little Spring can be seen from the beach behind the piling bulkhead to the east of Lot #1 South Beach Annex. While from conception to completion the water system took 10 years plus to complete, Beckett Point now has adequate water and a fire suppression system.

Water Reservoir on South hillside at Tax Lot #2

Pump station near South Beach Annex #9

Fire equipment storage shed – Entrance to North Beach

Wooden wheeled pump and hose cart stored at fire shed

Beach bulkhead remnants at Little Spring East of South Beach Annex Lot #1

BECKETT POINT LOTS

Event records from the 1940's are sparse. In a letter, referencing historical events prior to 1950, Dorothy Plut relates the thought, "I am quite sure Mr. Seeley, a first secretary, did not take minutes, at least, we never saw any."

However, it is shown in records that original leases were established at $25 per lot along with a $5 annual fee. The club also shouldered the property tax burdens. This appears to have remained the case until 1951 when lot leases purchases moved to $50 per lot and could be paid in 10 yearly payments if desired. A $25 initial fee was established to join the club.

Also, in 1951, a committee was selected to plot the lots of the corporation, establish baselines, permanently mark and make a map of these. Leases were made out to expire March 1, 1984 with an optional renewal at 45 years, providing lessor corp. is still in existence. Club joining fee at this time was $25, water assessment $15, electric assessment of $30 payable at installments of $15 for two years. Dues were $5 per year. Permission was granted to construct garages on the lagoon side of the road and immediately to the rear of the beach lots. Buildings were to be 10 feet from the edge of the road with a 25 foot width and a 12 foot height limit. Fill for any proposed garages was to come from the hill behind Lot #9 South Beach Annex and to the South towards Lot #1. In 1953, South Beach Annex #3 owner Reverend Mather was contacted by the club and informed that the hillside to the rear of his lot would have considerable fill removed for filling, raising and grading the road and adjacent lagoon and beach sideways. His benefit would be a nice road turn around space to the rear of the lot. As a result today we have the turn around and parking area at the south end of Beckett Point road.

Money problems arose in 1955, due to a decrease in lease payments and increase in expenses. A drive to increase the membership base was instituted. Assessed values had greatly increased from 1951 to 1955. Membership was made aware that the land the corporation bought in 1939 was now valued at $50,000 therefore membership dues were increased from $5 to $8 per year. In 1956 club sold lot leases were increased to $100 payable at $10 per year if so wished. Lots with wooden bulkheads were set at $150 for any lot repossessed by the club. Water assessments were $15, electrical assessments $30, wood bulkheads $90, concrete bulkheads $160 and a joining fee of $25 and annual dues of $8.

Tracking club values:

Excerpts from January 18, 1951 trustees meeting disclosed the value of corporation property based on actual costs at the time of acquisition.

Lot 1 Section 23	$1,000
Lot 2 Section 23	1,000
Lot 3 Section 23	500
Water and fire system:	6,381
Platform Scales	28
Boat Ways	350
Total	$9,259

1972 the club evaluation by the county was raised from $75,000 (tax bill #840) to evaluation of $554,350 at 28 ml level. This was protested by the membership and evaluation was reduced to $354,000. In partial this reduction was accomplished by placing the forested area into a tree farm status. Dues at this time were raised from $20 to $30.

1953 the road to access Beckett Point was greatly improved. The road from Chevy Chase was rebuilt and oiled to and around the club grounds. Five new cottages were established in this year now showing 57 cottages, 3 garages, 140 active members and 10 inactive members.

Subsequent to 1958 it had been established that lot lines were identified before lots were to be transferred, however they were often vague and sometimes in dispute. In 1958 a scale map was approved for the boundaries of club property showing in detail all lot lines, building lines, bulkhead lines, county roads, club roads, community areas, and utility and property lines. The map was approved June 10, 1958 and henceforth known as the official plot of Beckett Point grounds. Any controversy was to be resolved by the map. The map was to be kept up to date with changes or additions as needed.

With the plot map of 1958 in place lot lines became more defined, however disputes continued to arise. In June, 1969 it was established that clear lot lines must be in place before transfer to a new member. While some lending institutions were eager to loan on the value of the lot lease alone it was becoming clear most were requiring more documentation of boundary lines and financing was being denied.

During the mid 1990's the club chose to establish a boundary committee, resolve lot line disputes, and make the lot boundaries permanent and recorded. After a long extended effort by the club member lot committee, the option was given to members to establish the four corner markers and sign a line agreement with their neighbor. Those choosing so would have them surveyed and recorded. During this time frame the sewer project (BPFC LOSS) was being formulated. It became evident that for completion of the sewer, lot boundaries would have to be firmly established ensuring non encroachment of sewer infrastructure. The club determined all lots would be surveyed. Disputes were resolved, neighbor's lines agreed upon and the survey accomplished and recorded in the Jefferson County records. Overall this project encompassed a number of years of effort with many club members involved at different times.

However, due to particular diligent members Margaret Palo, Keith Hansen, Bill Smith, Betsy Lee, Patti Sahlinger and Kathy Poole, this project finally came to a close and Beckett Point is now platted, surveyed and recorded.

It is interesting to note the progression of cabin construction at the point. Many of the early cabins were constructed of salvage from the beach, with improvement over the times. Others were transported in. West Beach #28/29 was originally the top story of a fire station and transported to Beckett Point. West Beach #4, 9 and 10 were salvage cabins transported by barge from Port Townsend. South Beach #18 was transported from Adelma Beach. South Beach Annex #21 and 37/38 were catalog kits. West Beach #8 displays the ingenuity of a true craftsman with its unique construction. Each home shows its own style making Beckett Point a community unlike few others.

SEWER SYSTEM

June 15, 1988 City water arrived at Beckett Point. During the nearly 50 years of development at Beckett Point the environmental concerns arose, and shortly after water arrived it began to be addressed. The water system took some years from concept thoughts to the taps being turned on. At the onset, the membership knew that a sewer project would be to date the club's most ambitious undertaking. It turned out to be a project that required massive input of member's time, financial commitment and unforeseen hurdles and on completion has defined an impact on similar communities in Puget Sound.

At the July 1989 meeting the BPFC sewer system was first addressed. Neighboring Ocean Grove community was in Phase 2 of implementing a sewer system through the PUD. A committee was formed to focus on such a project at Beckett Point. At issue was BPFC potential for members' residences individual system failures. The extent of many systems was unknown and due to the points geographical profile systems failures could have a catastrophic effect on our biggest resource, our water. This could have a dramatic effect on our community; thusly this project was taken most seriously by the membership.

During the pursuing 10 years committees came and went. Types of systems were investigated, finding was always on the front burner and the relationship with the Jefferson County PUD was instituted. In December 2001 the PUD began the process to initiate investigating studies and research necessary to form a utility district to construct, own and operate a drain field at Beckett Point.

In 2003 the community was informed that Washington Dept of Health, while conducting a shoreline shellfish survey around Discovery Bay, had recommended that Beckett Point be placed in a concerned status due to potential lack of treatment in gravity fed systems. Their recommendation highlighted the urgency to move forward. Design, engineering, and a permitting process were put forward. The project became known at the Beckett Point Large Onsite Septic System (LOSS).

In November 2006 a proposal to regulatory agencies was drafted and submitted. The proposal included design and construction of a large onsite septic system (LOSS) for BPFC thus eliminating individual systems and creating a community collection and treatment system, eliminating potential pollution of nearby waters. The system involved abandoning individual systems and creating community sewage collection and an onsite treatment. Individual residences, grinder pump stations, collect sewage and convey to underground pump stations and ultimately deliver to two septic tanks located on the eastern portion of BPFC property. The effluent then is pumped to large drain fields. The septic tank and drain field encompass approximately five acres.

After, what at times appeared to be insurmountable obstacles overcome by considerable effort by members working on this project, funding was obtained. State and private loans were submitted. The original cost portrayed in the early project phase had doubled and the construction start up stood at an estimated 2.8 million dollars or approximately $28,000 per hook up. The bidding process was completed, construction began during early 2007.

The project proceeded with few unanticipated problems, being approximately 1/3 completed when on May 27, 2007 excavating unearthed archeological remains of Native Americans 100 years or older.

In 1953, Cape George Fishermen's, Inc. quit claimed to Jefferson County a 40 foot access road through the community. It was on this road near the boat ramp that these remains were found.

Excavation came to a halt and the PUD called in archeologists to evaluate the site. Chain length fence covered with tarps (for privacy) were installed while archeologist, tribal members, sifted through excavated material and sought to find additional remains and artifacts. The Jamestown S'Klallam tribe revealed that Beckett Point was a former village site. The archeological site study primarily was funded by grants from the Washington State Dept of Archeological and Historic Preservation. Near the end of June close monitoring at excavation areas was put in place and work proceeded again. During the winter of 2007/2008 residence systems came in service and the project completed within the original cost estimates.

From initial system discussions to flush was nearly two decades. This was accomplished through persistent and dedicated commitment of members. Along with peace of mind over potential sewage pollution BPFC has set an example for other Puget Sound communities to address their own situations.

Construction project unearths remains

Beckett Point is an 85-acre development on a sand spit that juts into Discovery Bay about 10 miles west of Port Townsend. The area may include a cemetery, a Skokomish tribal official said.

NEAR PORT TOWNSEND | The discovery of 58 human bone fragments, believed to be of Native Americans, has stopped work on a sewer-system project on a private development.

BY LYNDA V. MAPES
Seattle Times staff reporter

The discovery of human remains has turned a construction job in a private development near Port Townsend into a crash course in the history of the area's first people.

The project at Beckett Point, an 85-acre development on a sand spit that juts into Discovery Bay about 10 miles west of Port Townsend, was shut down following the discovery last month of about 58 human bone fragments by contractors digging a sewer system.

Last week, more remains were found when an archaeologist screened backfill from the same trench. The remains are believed to be those of Native Americans who might have used the area as a seasonal camp, said Tom Strong, deputy manager at the Skokomish Tribe.

Archaeologists have also found fire-cracked rock and midden — dark, oily ground, with remains from cooking and food preparation that are often a first sign of human use and settlement.

It is possible the area also includes a cemetery, Strong said. But there's no way to know until a full archaeological survey of the site is completed, perhaps within a month.

Please see > **BECKETT, B4**

MARK HARRISON / THE SEATTLE TIMES

A study team processes material from the site at Beckett Point where human remains were discovered. Besides the bone fragments, archaeologists have also found fire-cracked rock and midden — dark, oily ground, with remains from cooking and food preparation that are often a first sign of human use and settlement.

< Beckett
FROM B1

CONSTRUCTION PROJECT UNEARTHS BONE FRAGMENTS

Concern over costs: "I worry every time they dig a hole"

In the meantime, some work has restarted in an area away from the initial find.

The Beckett Point community has been around since 1939, and is owned by the nonprofit Beckett Point Fisherman's Club. About 162 people lease property from the club.

The club decided about seven years ago to replace aging septic tanks that were believed to be polluting Puget Sound. Homeowners had no idea then an archaeological discovery would become part of the bargain, said Keith Hansen, president of the homeowners' association.

"You have mixed feelings; it's interesting to learn the history that is right in your back yard," Hansen said.

But residents are now also worried about the costs of the project escalating. Homeowners are already paying about $28,000 each for the hook-ups. Now some aren't sure what the bottom line will be. "I worry every time they dig a hole," Hansen said. "Other communities are looking at this, and it may affect their willingness to do this kind of work."

The state and county may offer some grants to help defray the archaeological costs. Tribes are also contributing cultural and archaeological experts.

Cooperation has been extensive, Strong said. He credits a legacy of working together by Jefferson County elected officials and staff in the shared Quilcene and northern Hood Canal watershed.

Strong said he only wished talk about the site had started sooner. The project got its permits before Gov. Christine Gregoire issued an executive order in 2005 that would have required an archaeological survey. None was done prior to construction.

Still, even a survey might have missed remains. "We don't have X-ray vision," cautioned Allyson Brooks, director of the state Department of Archaeology and Historic Preservation.

Meanwhile, a similar concern last week in Port Angeles turned out to be unfounded. Work on a $13.8 million downtown transit site was halted briefly when bones were found, but archaeologists determined the remains were the butchered bones of a cow, said Mark Madsen, city manager.

Lynda V. Mapes: 206-464-2736 or lmapes@seattletimes.com

 Information

BECKETT POINT FISHERMAN'S CLUB: http://beckettpoint.com/beckett/home.aspx

Evidence clear, archaeologist says of findings

By Jeff Chew
Peninsula Daily News

DISCOVERY BAY — Native American remains uncovered last week at Beckett Point probably predate recorded history.

"We have reason to believe that there are remains of prehistoric people here," archaeologist Gary Wessen said Monday at the Beckett Point dig site near the community's boat ramp overlooking Discovery Bay.

"There certainly is evidence that [Native American] people were here."

Wessen, who was hired by Jefferson County Public Utility District and the state Department of Archaeology and Historic Preservation, said work at the site would probably wrap up today.

Wessen was reluctant to detail what has been found so far, saying he preferred to wait until he and his archaeological team of tribal members had completed the task of disinterring remains.

Turn to Beckett/A4

Beckett: More remains found

CONTINUED FROM A1

He did say that more than one set of remains has been exhumed.

He said he first wanted to hear from the tribes, including Jamestown S'Klallam and Port Gamble S'Klallam, for their comments.

"I will talk more when I actually understand what the story is here," he said.

Native burial grounds

Known for more than 40 years is that Beckett Point and part of the Discovery Bay shore were Native American burial grounds, he said, citing an excerpt from the book, *With Pride in Heritage: History of Jefferson County*.

The historic account was published in 1966 by the Jefferson County Historical Society and is now out of print.

"The graveyard at the head of Discovery Bay was originally an Indian burial ground," the book states. "Beckett Point was another."

During the latter half of last week and on Monday, the team has reopened a trench that the PUD's contractor had dug as part of a $2.8 million Beckett Point community septic and drainfield system.

The team has been carefully sifting through dug-up soil alongside Beckett Point Road, where it enters the lower village where about 80 residences along the shoreline have failing septic systems.

The team last week sifted through backfill piles directly across Beckett Point Road where the PUD contractor, Pape and Sons, was digging a trench when remains were unearthed in late May.

That stopped work on the Beckett Point septic and drainfield system — although state officials allowed PUD to continue work on the upper hillside section of the project last week, while the archaeological team worked below near the shore.

No other remains or artifacts have been uncovered at the uphill portion of the project off Beckett Point Road.

The project is intended to replace septic systems for about 100 homes, 80 of which are failing along the shoreline and threatening to pollute shellfish-rich Discovery Bay.

While laying pipeline for the PUD project in late May, 58 bone and bone fragments were uncovered and turned into Jefferson County Sheriff's Office.

Assistant State Archaeologist Stephenie Kramer, with the state Department of Archaeology and Historic Preservation, at the time stated that initial findings showed the remains were believed to be those of a Native American, 100 years or older.

TURN TO BECKETT/A5

Beckett: Grants received

CONTINUED FROM A4

The agency then informed PUD officials that disturbing Native graves without a permit from state Archaeology is a Class C felony.

Wessen is expected to evaluate the situation this week and submit a plan of action to the Department of Archaeology and Historic Preservation.

Wessen has worked on other Peninsula archaeological digs, including Ozette, a 1700s Makah village on the West End coast, and the most recent discovery — 2,700-year-old Tsewhit-zen on Port Angeles Harbor.

Ancestors of the Lower Elwha Klallam tribe were discovered in 2003 at the site of the Hood Canal Bridge graving yard then under construction.

The Lower Elwha tribe and archaeologists exhumed more than 300 burials and unearthed thousands of artifacts before the tribe asked the state Department of Transportation to halt the project in December 2004.

The Jefferson PUD most recently received a $10,000 grant from state Archaeology for continued inspection of the Beckett Point section.

With the help of Jefferson County officials PUD seeks more state grant dollars, instead of loans, that could come through Gov. Chris Gregoire's Puget Sound Initiative, or anther source.

The governor's initiative, which renewed Sunday, aims to clean up the region's waterways. The Legislature this year approved $238 million to fund such projects.

A grant written by Mike McNickle and the Jefferson County Health Department was submitted to the state Department of Ecology on Friday.

The $250,000 grant titled, "Jefferson County Shellfish Protection, Water Quality Improvement and Significant Archaeological/Cultural Remains Preservation Demonstration Project," would help pay for completion of archaeological work at Beckett Point.

It would also help pay for other county projects relating to water quality, including a proposed Tri-Area sewer system, county officials said.

Port Townsend-Jefferson County Editor Jeff Chew can be reached at 360-385-2335 or jeff.chew@peninsuladailynews.com.

'Prehistoric' remains at Beckett

JEFF CHEW/PENINSULA DAILY NEW

Tribal members led by archaeologist Gary Wessen expect to wrap up their preliminary exploration dig at Beckett Point today.

Drain field site preparation

Completed and operational drain field

One of two pump station sites

DISCOVERY BAY TIDELANDS & RECREATION

The founders formed Cape George Fishermen's Inc to provide a recreational area in which to stimulate interest in salt water fishing and provide for competition. In the early days, Discovery Bay and surrounding waters provided an abundance of bounty. Bottom fish were plentiful and the annual returning salmon runs lead to many successful fishing trips. In the 40's, the boat launching system was comprised of tails and rollers at many of the member cabins. This later led to a more sophisticated rail/dolly system with a gasoline powered winch and in 1952 when electricity arrived an electric powered winch was installed. This was used as a community launching facility and saw heavy use when the runs were in and, in particular, on derby days.

Along North beach a float and dock was constructed allowing tie up sites and skiff pullout. In 1956 the boat ramp was constructed originally being 60 feet x 10 feet and in 1963 was extended by an additional 30 feet. As time went on, storms took their toll on the dock and in 1964 docks on the beach were banned.

In the late 50's the railway system was dismantled leaving the boat ramp as the means to launch boats. Today, a club member oversees maintenance and upkeep on our ramp.

Keeping with the original articles, competition has been a large part of life at Beckett Point. Records show in the 1950's derbies held on July 4th and Labor Day had 60 plus entrants. Early day derby winner's records are sparse. However, in later years winners names of club members show up including Tom Plut, Linda Allen, Al Martin, William Arey, Bert Carr, Lorraine Meyers, Evelyn Marcelo, Mable Eronimo, John Meyers, Dennis Ankeny and Bill Sahlinger. It took catch weights of 20 plus pounds generally to win. An interesting note is that during the 40's and early 50's an award of $10 was given to the largest fish caught by male and female for the year. Club minutes show this was discontinued in 1956 due to discontent and lack of harmony of the membership. Evidently a winner's dispute arose. By the late 80's fish numbers were waning and derby attendance was suffering.

In 1984 our summer derby had 18 entrants with first place at 13 lbs and second at 11 lbs. The derbies success and continuance varied until 1996 when Bill Sahlinger and Dan Maloney made a conceited effort to revive the derbies. In 1989 Ed Edwards and his wife put together BPFC first annual kids fishing derby. In 1994 Dan Maloney became the kids' derby chairman and kids' and adults' derbies were held together for a time.

In 2000 the kids' derby became catch and release. By 2004 state fishing openings and lack of returning runs led to a cessation of Beckett Point's organized derbies. The local President's Day three-day derby continues to draw a large number of fisher people and many participants can be seen using the club boat ramp during this derby.

In staying with our corporation's declared purpose for being, BPFC has always been a leader in Puget Sound Resource Preservation. As early as 1953 the club has participated in conservation projects. At this time Cape George Fishermen's Inc joined Port Townsend Salmon Club, Olympic Conservation Association and the Washington Sports Council in a movement to regulate commercial fishing in Discovery Bay during sport fishing season.

In the 80's during hearings on issuing fish pen farming licenses in Discovery Bay, Beckett Point club members largely participated and had a major voice in the licenses being denied. The overwhelming evidence of Puget Sound environment harm was too great for members not to be heard. The club continues to monitor and participate in all matters reflecting Discovery Bay water quality.

In July, 1940 a seafood growing company by the name of Johnson and Gunstone, with headquarters on the South shore of Discovery Bay purchased the tidelands of second class from the State of Washington. Affecting Beckett Point this meant tidelands from the point easterly along club property were no longer available to club members for certain usage.

On August 26, 1952 Cape George Fishermen's Inc. purchased the tidelands along Beckett Point's westerly shore, from the point northwesterly through North beach. The amount paid was $2043.25. On the club's application to the State of Washington Public Lands for appraisement and sale of state tidelands it was noted that this tideland fronts on property now owned by this organization and beach rights are desirable to assure members access to boat mooring and landings.

In 1954 the Gunstone Company notified the club that further clam digging on their tidelands would not be allowed. In 1974 the issue of boat beach usage arose again as the Gunstone Company threatened to allow no access to the beach (violators would be cited for trespassing). At this time club discussion turned to purchasing or leasing beach rights from Gunstone. No productive agreement was reached. The issue of tideland usage continued to surface and in September, 1992 member Jack Meyer in a report to the club concluded the following:

"The tidelands of the second class beginning at the point South along club property are owned by Johnson and Gunstone pursuant to their purchase from the State of Washington in July, 1940 (Deed #17563). Tidelands of the second class are defined by Chapter 255 of the Sessions Law of 1927. Tidelands of second class reach from low low water to mean high tide. Roughly this is as far out as the tide ever goes upward to approximately to 7.2 feet at Beckett Point. This mean is corrected by the U.S. Coast and Geodetic survey every 18 years. A good reference pamphlet was printed by Chicago Title Insurance Company entitled "Waterfront titles in the State of Washington. The State of Washington is a non/riparian state. Simply put, this means the state has control over all the waters. The state only may control access to the waters and the State of Washington does not bar the public from use of the waters."

In accordance with the law and the ownership of these tidelands by Johnson and Gunstone, other than access of the water, no beach activities are allowed by the members or the public between the low low and high mean. No beach digging is allowed and activities such as beach fires, wood cutting, etc. shall be above the mean high tide point.

Often at low tide times Gunstone Company employees can be observed harvesting shellfish in this vicinity. In 2005 a commercial geoduck fanning operation commenced approximately 1-1/2 miles south of the point. These aqua farmers have been very gracious in answering questions and explaining their farming procedures to inquiring beach walkers. Beckett Point Fishermen's club members take great pride in maintaining the tidelands in every environmentally correct way, thus continuing to be in compliance with our original Articles of Incorporation.

During the spring of 2013, Gunstone Co. and BPFC reached agreement for purchase of tide lands Sec. 23-Lot #1. The new area basically goes from the point to SPA Lot #18. The sales price was $16,600 and was financed through a $125 per lot membership assessment.

Participants in the Beckett Point Kids' Fishing Derby landed more than 25 fish, Sept. 3. The $50 first prize went to Michael Phillips with a 4 pound, 13 ounce dog fish. Special recognition was given to Ashley Ross for a 2 pound 3 ounce salmon. The Sportsman's Award went to James Pedersen who caught and released a 70-pound out-of-season halibut. The top ten winners were Michael Phillip, Sarah Barber, Mary Ann Madsen, Alicia Ross, Sondra Habercorn, Jennifer Ratcliff, Nicole Edwards, Tiffany Habercorn and Ashley Ross.

The Port Townsend/Jefferson County Leader
B-2—Wednesday, Sept. 6th, 1989

Successful pot pull

Left to Right: Kirby Sooy, Jack Freeman, Bert Carr

Taken in the 1950's

Back Row Left to Right:
Ted Gunterrnan, Ed Dupuis, Roy Movius, Carl Hane, Walt Johnson, Doc Werner, Bruce Blevins, Mrs. Mc Ilroy, Grace DeLeo, Tony DeLeo, Herb Bromley, Tom Glen
Front Row Left to Right:
Sgt. Cole, Walt Meyers, Barney Mullaney, Ivan Barnett, Joe Steve

Left to Right:
George Robertson (Margaret Carr's uncle), Unknown Woman (last name Slinko?), Cecil Guptill (Joy Guptill's father)

Bert Carr (Margaret Carr's father)

Left to Right:
Bert Carr, Carl Haines *In front of the store* that Carl Haines owned

Left to Right:
Margaret Carr, Barbara Gauthier, (Leonard) Roberta Carr (Enders) *Taken about 1943 by the current boat ramp. Notice dock/pilings* to *the float in the background.*

PLAYGROUND

Helen Marriott of the Plut family recalls the fine memories of softball games played on long summer evenings at Beckett Point. "Kids, young and old, families from all parts of the beach would show up. There was a special rule for little ball players that allowed them to keep swinging the bat until they hit the ball". The point was a community that helped one another, played and fished together, and enjoyed summer bliss.

Happening in the 1960's the road around the point was repositioned and today's club common area was filled, improved and leveled to today's look. No building was allowed between lots West Beach 7 and South Beach 5 on lagoon side. In August 2000 the lagoon and commons area were designated as level 3 wetlands. Activities were held on the site and in the late 90's Dennis Ankeny and Gene Burke provided the kid's boat and the teeter totter. In 2002 the club authorized and permits were granted for construction of today's split log table and the log covering known as BPFC Clubhouse. With material costs of $20,000, committee members Dennis Ankeny and Gene Burke provided the club with our fine facilities. Throughout the year club members can be found using this area and on July 4th our annual community picnic is a place for members to catch up and renew friendships with fellow neighbors.

Bill Smith's "Pride & Joy"

July 4th Parade

July 4th, 2013

BULKHEADS

Prior to 1952 bulkheads were put in place by some leaseholders and others chose not to. Also, it is interesting that prior to this time lot shuffling was common. If a leaseholder decided he would rather occupy a different available lot a switch was made. Also, when a foreclosed lot occurred the adjoining leaseholders were given first choice to acquire. After that it was put out to market. Also, it is noted that with the closure of Fort Warden, a loss of some 2500 population and payroll resulting in property depreciating in value in this area and club records show lots being abandoned and/or foreclosed on were not uncommon.

The winter of 1951 brought a series of severe storms and a large over tide created much damage to the point.

In 1952 the membership voted all lots would have a suitable bulkhead in place. If not done by the leaseholder the club will contract, address, and assess costs against the lots. Bulkhead requirements were for wood 10 inch minimum top, 4 feet below the beach and 3 feet above. Cement bulkheads would be 8 inch top, 3 feet below the beach and 3 feet above. Billings to the leaseholders for bulkheads constructed by the club per lot were $90 for the wooden type and $160 for concrete. They were financed through three annual payments with 6% interest. At this time a beach log salvage operation was in the area and logs were gathered, towed to Beckett Point and left on the beach for bulkhead material. During the winter of 2001/2002 substantial beach erosion occurred at the point and near the boat ramp. Boulder sized rocks were installed in the affected areas. Today the bulkhead requirement is an integral part of life at Beckett Point. Leaseholders must maintain their bulkheads and a committee of members monitors bulkhead conditions.

February 4th, 2006

BECKETT POINT FLOOD—This is how a portion of the Beckett Point summer home colony looked Saturday after a high tide storm washed a large accumulation of logs and debris clear over the south beach and deposited it in the lagoon. Visible (lower center) is a cabin boat owned by Chet Gillett, which was carried from the beach at extreme left into the lagoon with the logs. The road, completely under water, follows the line of power poles at the left. (Burdette Redding photos.)

We found the missing beach driftwood

Beckett Point over tide

FLAG POLE

In 1999 Greg Moga was able to obtain a salvage utility light pole from a site near Ballard.

The pole was transported to Enumclaw and vamped to a flag pole, then transported to Beckett Point. Club members erected the pole in the spring of 2000. Gene Burke, Greg Moga and a club work team laid the foundation and raised the pole. Jer Reeves arranged for the Founder's plaque and the monument materials were donated by Shine quarry. On July 4, 2000 the flag was raised having been donated by Dick and Glenda Cable in memory of Glenda's parents, Cliff and Bea Swain, club members since 1959.

In 2001, the early Founder's plaque was installed noting the founding date 6-27-39 and naming founders:

Lyle Arey
Bruce Blevins
Bert Carr
Roy Dale
Cecil Guptill
H. L. Hutzler
S.P. Lockhart
N.W. Raynor

Margaret Palo at flagpole dedication

Northern Transport, Inc - Transporting flagpole

Dick and Glenda (Swain) Cable raising the flag at dedication ceremony

Beckett Point Rare Prairie Habitat

Most of us are well aware of the unique piece of Jefferson County that we are privileged to occupy. Many of us have grown up here, exploring the pebbly shore; initially turning over rocks for small crabs, sand fleas, sand dollars and agates, but quickly advancing to fishing for salmon and lingcod or digging for littlenecks and horse clams. We heard the stories about the first human visitors to this little point - my grandmother, Lois Easton, told of the Indians that summered on its shore using hair from the now extinct white dogs for their winter blankets. And, when we set about to protect our lovely bay from our increasingly failing septic tanks we heard of the "discovery" of ancient Native American remains found at our boat ramp.

But, some of us may not know of the *other* unique piece of land we own high above the point nestled among the firs and peeking out from the "balds". This parcel is so rare that it represents a time before we arrived, even before the Indians arrived. This parcel represents the Quimper Peninsula in its pre-settlement prairie habitat state.

"Prairie" remnants are one of Washington State's rarest of habitats. Washington Natural Heritage Program, Washington Native Plant Society, Jefferson Land Trust, Washington Department of Fish and Wildlife, and the USDA are just some of the local state and federal organizations hoping to preserve such habitats before they are completely eradicated by encroaching development or invasive plants. Nestled on the hillside of Beckett Point Fishermen's Club is a rare example of a local natural prairie area that has been spared from development impacts. Kah Tai Prairie Preserve, a tiny piece located within the city limits, is another example of this rare prairie habitat.

What makes our special place worth preserving is disclosed below in a 1990 letter written to Jefferson Land Trust.

> "As you look over the enclosed Beckett Point plant list (the result of several years of field work by Nelsa Buckingham and other members of the Olympic Peninsula Chapter of the Washington Native Plant Society) you will notice those plants which we refer to as "prairie indicators" marked with an asterisk (*). So far, we have discovered 13 of these indicator species. I am certain that future field work will uncover more such indicators. At this point, I want to single out two of these species for special consideration, namely *Opuntia fragilis,* our native prickly pear cactus, and *Phacelia linearis,* the threadleaf phacelia. Fossil pollen grains of *Opuntia fragilis* were uncovered at the Manis Mastodon archaeological she near Sequim, indicating this cactus was a part of the pioneer vegetation 11,000 ago, colonizing fleshly deglaciated terrain on the northeastern Olympic Peninsula. Today, coastal populations of *O. fragilis* extend northward through the San Juan Islands to the east of the mountains on Vancouver Island but are known at only two locations on the Olympic Peninsula - the Sequim area and Beckett Point. The Sequim population has been decimated by development (including irrigation of the former prairie soils) and is represented today by a few small fragments.
>
> The Beckett Point population, on the other hand, is in good shape. In addition to the rare prairie assemblage found at Beckett Point, including the presence of a healthy *Opuntia* population, there is also what constitutes the last remaining stand of old growth conifers on the Quimper Peninsula. Because the dominant trees are dwarfed and deformed, and exist on very steep slopes, they have never been logged. The surviving stand represents essentially the same forest type observed by the Vancouver expedition in t792 when it anchored for some weeks in Discovery Bay. In fact, the first botanist to note the presence of

> *Opuntia* at this northern latitude was the great Scottish surgeon and naturalist Archibald Menzies, who accompanied this expedition. It is also significant to note that the Douglas fir/ocean spray/snowberry plant community characteristic of the Beckett Point site is one of the "elements" *(Pseudotsuga-Holodiscus-Symphoricarpos)* that the Washington Natural Heritage Program lists as a high priority that still lacks any protected example.
>
> Finally, it is also noteworthy that a population of the Northwestern fence lizard *(Sceloporus occidentalis)* can be found at this site, a locally rare and disjunct population which also used to be seen at some sites in Port Townsend but has since disappeared, probably due to domestic cat predation."

In 2005, the Beckett Point board recognized the significance of this prairie habitat and formed The Stewardship committee to explore options for protection. A letter from Anita McMillan, WDFW botanist, describes well the stewardship required to preserve this significant parcel.

> "We are very interested in the unique prairie-cactus habitat that exists at Beckett Point. My main concern with the Beckett Point prairie site would be to determine if there is a way to control the invasive plants that will over time change the site and degrade its condition. Scotch broom was the obvious invasive, but there are certainly others not so obvious (invasive grasses that are not prairie species, and over time they change the soil conditions away from prairie conditions). It is such that the soil conditions are best when in a depleted state for prairie plants. They thrive in these conditions because they can compete well. When invasive plants become established the soil becomes richer and the prairie plants can't compete. The best way this happened in ages past was with fire. Without fire as a tool we struggle with ways to manage these sites."

In May 2007 Beckett Point, in coordination with WDFW, began removing 3 large areas of scotch broom and small conifers that were encroaching on the prairie habitat. At the same time, two visits were made by a WDFW researcher surveying for the Taylor's checkerspot butterfly, listed as a Washington endangered species.

Ms. McMillan wrote to the Stewardship committee again:

> "We would certainly like to continue monitoring the site for butterflies and the unique prairie plants that occur there. There may end up being other invertebrates that should be monitored there as well. Thanks for your keen stewardship for this site. I applaud your involvement and encourage you to continue learning and supporting the best practices for management of this habitat."

As we continue to "discover" and re-discover the unique attributes our founders recognized on our special point on Discovery Bay, we are challenged to continue to protect and steward its waters, forests, balds, wetlands, and shores for our children's children.

Submitted by,
Connie Ross
Stewardship Committee

Beckett Point Rare Prairie Habitat

VASCULAR PLANTS OF BECKETT POINT

S24, T3ON, R2W
(Tax Lot #3, 17.50 Ac.)
Steep, south-facing bluffs on Discovery Bay; 150' elevation; very unstable soils (gravelly, sandy loam).

* = prairie indicator
(ALIEN) = non native plant

Achillea millefolium ssp. Lanulosa	Yarrow
Allium acuminatum	Tapertip onion
Amelanchier alnifolia var. semiintegrifolia	Serviceberry
*Arabis hirsuta var. glabrata	Hairy rockcress
Arbutus menziesii	Madrona
Arenaria macrophylla	Bigleaf sandwort
Arteinisia suksdorfii	Suksdorfs sage
*Brodiaea coronaria ssp. Coronaria	Harvest brodiaea
Bromus diandrus (ALIEN)	Ripgut
Bromus pacificus	Pacific brome
Bromus sitchensis var. sitchensis	Alaska brome
Bromus tectorum (ALIEN)	Cheatgiass
Carex inops	
*Castilleja hispida var. hispida	Harsh paintbrush
*Cerastium arvense var. viscidulum	Field chickweed
Clarkia ainoena var. lindleyi	Farwell-to-spriiig
Crepis capillaris (ALIEN)	Smooth hawksbeard
Cytisus scoparius (AlIEN)	Scot's broom
Daetlyis glomerata (ALIEN)	Orchard grass
*Danthonia californica	California danthonia
*Delphinuijm menziesii	Menzies larkspur
Elymus glaucus	Blue wildrye
Equisetum laevigatum	Smooth scouring-rush
Eriophyllum lanatum var. leueophyllum	Woolly sunflower
Eiythroniutn oregonum	Giant fawnlily
Festuca idahoense	Idaho fescue
Festuca occidentalis	Western fescue
*Fritillaria lanceolata	Chocolate lilly
Galium aparine	Goosegrass
Gaultheria shallon	Salal
Geranium inolle (ALIEN)	Dovefoot geranium
Grindelia integrifolia var. inacrophylla	Gumweed
Habanaria elegans	Elegent rein orchid
Habanaria unalascensis	Alaska rein orchid

Hieracium albiflorum	White-flowered hawkweed
Holcus lanatus (ALIEN)	Velvet Grass
Holodiscus discolor	Ocean-spray
Hypochoeris radieata (ALIEN)	Hairy cat's ear
Koeleria cristata	Koeleria
*Lathyrus nevadensis	
ssp. lanceolatus var. pilosellus	Nuttall's pea
Lomatium nudicaule	Pestle parsnip
Lonicera ciliosa	Orange honeysuckle
Lonicera hispidula var. hispidula hairy honeysuckle	
Lotus micranthus	Small-flowered deervetch
Lupinus subvexus var. subvexus (ALIEN)	
Luzula campestris var. congesta	Field woodrush
Madia gracilis	Slender tarweed
Madia saLiva var. sativa	Coast tarweed
Mahonia aquafolium	Shining Oregon grape
Mahonia nervosa	Dull Oregon grape
Medicago sps.	Medic
*Montia perfoliata	Miner's lettuce
*Opuntia fragilis var. fragile	Prickly-pear cactus
Osmorhiza chilensis	Mountain sweet-eieely
*Phacelia linearis	Threadleafphacelia
Pseudotsuga menziesii var. menziesii	Douglas-fir
Pteridium aquilinum var. pubsecens	Bracken
*Ranunculus oceidentalis	
var. occidentalis	Western buttercup
Ribes sanguineum	
var. sanguineurn	Red-flowering current
Rosa gymnocarpa var. gymnocarpa	Baidhip rose
Rubus ursmus ssp. Macropetahis	Pacific blackberry
Rumex acetosella (ALIEN)	Sheep sorrel
Sanicula crassicaulis	
var. crassicaulis	
var. tripartite	Pacific sanicle
Sanicula bipinnatifida	Purple saniele
Satureja douglasii	Yerba Buena
Shepherdia canadensis	Buffalo-berry
Silene gallica (ALIEN)	Windmill pink
Sorbus aucuparia (ALIEN)	European mountain-ash
Stellaria media (ALIEN)	Chickweed
Symphoricarpos albus var. laevigatus	Common snowberry
Symphoricarpos mollis	Creeping snowberry
*Trifolium microcephalum	Small-head clover
Trifolium tridentatum	Tomcat clover
Verbascum thapsus (ALIEN)	Mullein

Vicia americana ssp. Americana   American vetch
Vicia gigantean   Giant vetch
Vicia hirsuta (ALIEN)   Hairy vetch
Vicia sativa (ALIEN)   Common vetch
Vulpia microstachys var. ciliata)
*Zigadenus venenosus
        var. venenosus   Deadly zigadcnus

Note: reptiles observed--Rubber boa (Charina bottae bottae), Northwestern Fence lizard (Sceloporus oceidentalis) and Alligator lizard (Gerrhonotus eoeruleus).

See following photos of our members in search of **Fritillaria lanceolata, Opuntia fragilis, Phacelia linearis, Sceloporus occidentalis, and Charina bottae boftae.**

Flora & Fauna on Rare Prairie Hike

Rubber Boa

Chocolate Lily

NW Fence Lizard

Threadleaf Phacelia

Prickly Pear Cactus

Club Members Rare Prairie Hike
In search of flora & fauna [See *Next Page*]

Jerry Gorsline, Diane Jones, Almeta Peterson, Diane Holmes

Jerry Gorsline, the Hutters, & Jill Larson

Jack Meyer & John Kennedy with Old Growth Conifer

LABOR DAY FIRE

On the afternoon of Monday, September 5th, 2011 (Labor Day), a fire broke out east of club members Dick and Glenda Cable's SBA Lot #1 home. It started very near the beach edge and quickly engulfed the old piling that protected the pipe that was previously used to transport water from the lower spring to the pump house near the turn around. Despite a number of member's efforts, it quickly spread uphill and into a full fledged, out of control fire. Fire crews from local jurisdictions responded and shortly thereafter the DNR took command. They basically set up three attack points: through the turn around, via the no longer used water storage area and southward downhill from the junction of Cape George Road and Discovery Bay Road. Helicopter water drops commenced around 7 pm and the fire was mostly contained shortly after dark. Residents of homes in the turnaround area spend most of the night watering their areas as the air was thick with flying burning embers. By dawn on September 6th, firefighters had made significant progress and mop-up tactics began. Timber fallers cut what burnt snags needed to come down and crews hand walked the entire area extinguishing hot spots. Around the clock hour surveillance stayed in effect until the end of the week as hot spots occasionally flared up.

The firefighters had set up camp at the Jefferson County Fairgrounds and upon wrap-up of the fir held s meeting to discuss events and suggestions for improvement. Attending BPFC members expressed their whole-hearted thanks and appreciation to all involved. While during this week there were few changes of light heartedness at the meeting everyone chuckled when it was noted that someone requested 250 hamburgers from a local fast food outlet and received dead silence followed by a dial-tone. Clearly an order or 250 hamburgers in Port Townsend was not necessary.

During the following winter of 2011/2012 a forester was hired to evaluate the burnt area. His consensus was other than some winter erosion we were in pretty good shape, as the fire did not get to much of the vegetation's root system and hillside growth should return. As of 2013 this had occurred and good coverage has happened. As time goes on members will keep watch of the burnt dead trees and address as needed. Perhaps these dead trees will, in fact, increase our wild life at the point. The beach entrance to the east of Lot #1 has been closed and the club posted signs that warned trees may come down. Fortunately it appears what rare Prairie Habitat was affected by the fire is recovering and will continue to be monitored. Prior to the fire on the hillside below the water tanks an extensive growth of invasive Scotch Broom has established itself and post-fire does not appear to be coming back. Hopefully this will continue as the area rebuilds itself.

wildfires cloud air

Fire burns 21 acres at Beckett Point

By James Robinson of the Leader

Three juveniles playing with fireworks on Labor Day were the cause of a blaze that, fanned by high winds, whipped across 21 acres of hillside above Beckett Point, say fire investigators. By Tuesday morning, however, emergency managers declared the fire contained.

"By contained, I mean that we have a dirt path around the fire, essentially boxing it in," said state Department of Natural Resources forester Pat Halford. "I use the word 'control' to describe the percentage of actual flames put out."

DNR personnel were among the nearly 100 firefighters from a number of area agencies who attacked the fire and kept the flames

See BECKETT, Page 9

Beckett: Fireworks caused 20-acre blaze

▼Continued from page 1

from reaching homes. No one was injured.

Although local fire crews from East Jefferson Fire Rescue, Port Ludlow Fire & Rescue and Clallam County 3 were first on the scene, the DNR personnel took command of the fire when the agency's crews arrived and a DNR firefighting helicopter from Chelan began an aerial attack about 7:20 p.m.

Bill Beezley, public information officer with East Jefferson Fire Rescue, said on Tuesday that DNR personnel remained on the scene to conduct mop-up operations and look for hot spots.

"About 50 DNR guys will walk the area foot by foot with infrared cameras searching for hot spots," Beezley said. "The primary blaze is out, and we're in pretty good shape, but EJFR is still on the periphery."

Beezley said the DNR helicopter also remained nearby on Tuesday morning to conduct additional water drops if necessary, but by 9:30 a.m. it had not been used.

Beezley estimated mop-up operations could take up to three days.

"I think they were fortunate to get it under control last night," Beezley said.

Despite two fires in the area – Beckett Point and the Big Hump Fire along the Duckabush River – Fran McNair, executive director of the Olympic Region Clean Air Agency, said that as of midday on Tuesday, air quality remains good in Port Townsend.

JUVENILE CHARGES

Jefferson County Sheriff Tony Hernandez said three juveniles, all younger than 18, had admitted to their roles in the accidental fire.

"When we spoke to the juveniles, they admitted what had happened," Hernandez said. "They were using a can of WD-40 to light bottle rockets. We'll probably forward this to the prosecutor's office and let them make a decision [on charges and prosecution]."

According to a witness, the fire "exploded" down the hillside above the fishing community as winds up to 20 mph whipped the flames. Fire personnel advised Beckett Point residents to evacuate the area, and some were separated from their homes for more than two hours as firefighters defended homes along the waterfront and attacked the fire from the ridge top, cutting fire lines around the blaze with hand tools and chainsaws.

On Sept. 5, firefighters came over the top of the ridge to keep flames from reaching the homes on the ridge overlooking Beckett Point. Photo by James Robinson

Despite scores of firefighters on the hillside, steep terrain hampered their efforts, and firefighters estimated the grade ranging from 35 to 80 percent. With footing difficult on the hillside, the DNR helicopter, which made eight to 10 water drops – along with decreasing winds – changed the game for firefighters.

"By about 5:30 p.m., winds had died down, and firefighters began gaining ground on the blaze," Beezley said.

"The crews made a couple of great saves on several homes," said EJFR Fire Chief Gordon Pomeroy. In some cases, flames came within 40 feet of several residences.

Firefighters from East Jefferson Fire Rescue, Port Ludlow Fire & Rescue and Naval Magazine Indian Island were joined by several 20-man hand crews from DNR.

Task force crews consisting of both career and volunteer firefighters also came from Clallam District 3 and Kitsap County fire departments. Crews from Fire Districts 2 (Quilcene) and 5 (Discovery Bay) provided medical support within District 1 while EJFR firefighters were at Beckett Point.

Beezley said he has no estimates of cost, but added that as soon as DNR arrives on a fire scene and takes command, it foots the bill from that point.

Firefighters on Sept. 5 kept this fireworks-induced wildfire from reaching homes on Beckett Point (the sea-level cabin community's southern edge, which is to the right) and the homes tucked into the tree line along Beckett Point Road. The fire started at about 3 p.m. on Monday, a result of kids playing with fireworks. Fickle winds fanned it to about 21 acres. It was 70 percent contained by 7 p.m. (This was the fire's calm section.) Soon after, helicopter began dropping water along ridge-top brush and trees. Photo by James Robinson

The Dock at North Beach
By Pat Maher

The club members agreed that a dock and "float" should be built for club member's use at Beckett Point. The visual and physical clutter of too many rail and pulleys systems that were now littering the beach attacked the Point's beauty like a creeping plague! The rails were hard to take care of, they were easy to trip over, they rusted, they collected seaweed that wasn't always cleaned up, and they were ugly to look at. And when members opted out of fishing, sold their place, or just lost interest, the rusting rails of east off mining carts, and other mechanical pressings and extrusions remained of the beach.

This was a time of the smaller boat. Clinker-built, lapstrake, and even a plank- board style, built upon "ribs" were as common as Fords. You could fish the choppy waters of Discovery Bay with an almost tattooed authority if your boat had a round bottom and a decent keel! They didn't develop the system of hauling boats to the beach from the comfort of your backyard, via boat trailer, until the late 1940's. Those early trailers were sometimes nothing more than a decent beam plopped across and errant auto axle. I think the "patrol" had fun with that issue! The idea for a "float" and attached dock had come. It would be a temporary holding spot for the many fisherman boats to rest between tides, or maybe go in for a lunch without having to beach, and thus, scratch and endanger your boat's hull.

Some members used the "Indian" anchoring system. That is where you took a light anchor, attached plenty of rope to hit the bottom, then you ran a long line from that anchor up the beach to an available log or bulkhead. Your boat was attached to the anchor. The anchor was attached to that long line up the beach. To activate the method, you placed the anchor gingerly on the bow plate of the boat. Then you gave a mighty shove to the boat, sending it to your choice of a resting place. At the appropriate moment, you pulled the anchor off the boat's bow plate, sending the anchor to the bottom. To retrieve the boat you used the beach line to tug the anchor to you and the boat hopefully came along. A float and dock would be the ideal project to build to help solve these anchoring and storage problems. Tugging a heavy boat up the beach on "rollers" was no fun. Tying up to a float would be much easier on the back and temperament. The time had come to build a dock and float.

Being that it sometimes blows a gale from the south at Beckett, it was decided to build this structure on North Beach. My grandfather, Peter Norby, consented to have it in front of his place at Lot 8 A. The main pilings were built of very lle3vily creosoted logs. Long 4" by 10" joists ran out on top of cross beams of considerable size. The main pilings were set in concrete bases. A very substantial hand railing ran the fill length and on both sides. The dock structure was about 5 feet wide and ran out about 75 feet.

The float itself was made of very large logs, maybe 5 or 6 in number. They were tied together with cross beams about 4" by 10". Planking was set on top of this. They even made a diving board on the sea-ward end for those hardy enough to try it! I did. Once.

The float decking had boat tie-up rails along the full length on both side. You could tie up your boat or even pull up small skiffs on top for awhile. Kids used to fish for bull heads and other assorted piscatorial delights. It was a busy place.

To get to the float from the dock, you walked down a long commercially made gangway. The gangway was "acquired" from the old government dock and warehouse at Diamond Point. The warehouse there supplied the Federal quarantine station located on Diamond Point when Washington State was only a territory. Later, during two world wars, the military added touches to the dock and warehouse. They put in the nice gangway that found its way to Beckett Point. I think the club got permission to "borrow" it. The end of the gangway had a roller on it so that it would roll back and forth with the raising and lowering of the tides. It sometimes squeaked. We would ignore it for a bit then someone would volunteer to go and deftly apply some much needed grease. It was usually my grandfather Pete Norby who would do it. In fact he took over the total maintenance of the float and dock system. Axel Swanson, who had lot 8, next to Norby's, would pitch in and do some of the duties.

One incident that affected the final look and quality of the dock was the U.S. Navy. Our military had, during WW. 2, decided to moor several large ammunition ships in Discovery Bay. They were anchored out about half a mile south of the point and on down to about Gunstone's clam digs and property. They were big, gray, and obnoxious. But we collared our contempt for this intrusion on the scenic beauty of the bay by telling ourselves that "it was for the war effort!" It even paid personal dividends for my grandparents. One day a landing barge was lowered off the ship with the ship's captain on board with his jeep. He landed right next to the dock where Grandpa Pete was sawing logs. Down came the bow of the landing craft and off came the jeep with the captain. Grandpa and the captain started talking, they went into the cabin and somehow a bottle of rye appeared. That resulted in boat trips out to the ship for dinner. I sat with the crew watching movies on the big deck, while my grandparents played cards with the captain. Grandma also was given "goodies" impossible to get by civilians during this war time such as real black pepper, and canned ham. I got free pie from the ship's bakery!

The ship's crew had a penchant for visiting various girls that spent the summer at the point. My aunt was one. About 4 girls and 4 sailors borrowed the ship landing craft for a moonlight cruise around the bay. As the girls jumped aboard, I was bribed by the sailors with a couple of those delightful pies to NOT tell what was going on. I didn't tell. The pies were appropriate payment for my silence! However, on thepr return near midnight, they crashed into the dock, re-routing the direction that the pilings were supposed to be pointing . Like up? They were now near horizontal. As was expected, the captain found out about this and with the threat of "keel-hauling" the errant crew, the next week the U.S. Navy repaired the dock. They did a wonderful job. It was even better than the original. Thus the touch of the military had left its print at Beckett Point!

The dock and float were used for many years by most people at Beckett. It was the starting point for those fabulous fishing derbies where great lunkers were brought in and hung on an overhead beam that also held the fish scale. The float was also the launching pad for many fireworks gatherings. For the 4th of July, beach parties, you could hang a sack of clams or crabs over the side of the float to keep them in the proper environment until the eating/cooking festivities started. But, alas, time took its toll. Not only did the dock and pier show the ravages of time, but Grandfather Peter Norby was showing age and aches. He lost interest in repairing the facility and so did everyone else. It became dangerous to walk on, no one wanted to do the winter haul-out of the large float, so it was thought best to "do it in." It was done in except for the concrete imbedded pilings. I have one picture of the last set of pilings, looking like a Japanese Tori with a dominant cross beam tying the two piling tops together, with the sun going down behind. I have the memories of the work and fin that was as commonplace as the tides.

Pat Maher
May 6, 2003

SOVIET SUBMARINE IN DISCOVERY BAY
FACT OR FICTION????

FACT: During the dates below noted in the Port Townsend Leader at about SBA #22/23 a section of beach some 100 feet in width and at about 0 foot tide simply disappeared. The beach had a hole some 2 feet deep and 100 feet long and out into the bay. No one could account for why this happened.

Gary Kinney, South Beach leaseholder at that time, after considerable research and communication with, as he called them, non-cooperative Military personnel gives a great deal of credence to the submarine in Discovery Bay theory. He theorizes the beach hole was a result of the subs underwater propeller wash and/or ballast pumping. Perhaps we will never know for sure the cause or validity of the Leader article but one can't help but wonder if maybe we were observed by a Soviet periscope.

8/23/2000 LEADER

Cold War in Discovery Bay

Editor, Leader:

The recent tragedy of the Russian submarine Kursk has kindled public interest in the stories of the Cold War submariner. In bits and pieces, the military history of this service emerges from secrecy. A pivotal episode of this history was a period of anti-submarine warfare conducted in the inland sea of Washington state.

On Dec. 7, 1984, the U.S. Navy brought a salvaged Soviet submarine to the waters off west central Whidbey Island. The sub was searched, intelligence gathered, and then it was scuttled in north Puget Sound.

A few days later the U.S. Navy would detect and trap a nuclear-powered Soviet attack submarine in Discovery Bay, west of Port Townsend. This event was marked on Dec. 13, when a Soviet submarine-launched anti-aircraft missile shot down a U.S. Navy EA-6B jet aircraft.

The crisis generated by this event would precipitate the Cold War's end.

(Hint for those of a historical bent: Read the December 1984 *New York Times*.)

MIKE MARSTON
Port Townsend

BECKETT POINT FOUND

I, Fred W. Mc Ilroy Jr. and my Dad, Fred W. Mc Ilroy Sr. was with the Discovery Party on a Saturday in September 1939 when we first walked down the beach from Cape George to review Beckett Point as a possible site for the club, a Group of Fishermen, fishing out of Cape George, with a Club House at that location, and a need for more room and fresh water.

Upon arriving at what is now the Boat Ramp area the party split into two groups, one group continued on down the beach and the second including myself went around the Lagoon on the hill side to the South Beach. On the North Beach the Group saw possible building sites for all of their members, a good low bank area to launch their boats, and in general a pleasant place to be. There is a lot of early history about the area, but at this time there was just an old fisherman's shack, now deserted, but a place when occupied by an old fishermen you could always count on a bowl of beans if you stopped by when on a hike on the beach. On the South side we saw an outlet to the Lagoon about midway down the beach, shallow, but flowing at the time we were there. To the East where the hillside towered over the beach spring water was flowing from low on the bill and those familiar with wells said there was enough to go with. After a thorough look at the two areas the two parties rejoined at the parting area and standing in a circle, had a discussion on the merits of the location.

At the end of the review someone stepped forward and said something like this; this is the place for us, the place for our children, and our children's children. There was a handshake across the circle by all. I think that they intended for this place to be a Family Heritage.

We do have a unique place here and there is only one other Group in the United States that is like us. It is Fair Hope, Alabama. You can access Fair Hope on the computer. They were organized in 1894 and are still going strong.

We have been going for a long time and I think we should continue our present course. Over the years we have worked our problems as they occur, such need for water, need for property lines, and need for septic system update for the environment. We have worked these in house and gone for advice outside when needed but have retained the integrity of our land to ourselves.

Our personal needs for land use are not all known, so we should retain all we have, and at present it is an excellent buffer for us.

The first Mc Ilroy cabin was built on the hill over Swede Row, was one of the few built before the road to Beckett Point existed. Most of the structural lumber was taken from the lot. The trees and saplings cut in clearing the area were used for the cabin base and framing. I do not remember the source of the cedar, but a free was used to cut the shingles used for siding and roofing on site. The remaining materials used were either carried by hand or dragged down the hill to the building shed. It was a time of neighbor helping neighbor and men volunteering to accomplish the task at hand. A composting type of toilet was installed in the house.

I believe the site on the bill was picked for the view of Diamond Point, Protection Island, and the beautiful sunsets in the evening. This cabin became a place for fishing, family gathering and a wonderful place for grandchildren.

Fred W. Mc Ilroy
1130 Beckett Point Road

The Building of a Cabin at Beckett Point

I was there in 1939 when we first surveyed Beckett Point as a place to relocate our club. When the place was selected I was away on an adventure that took me to the North Atlantic, Iceland, the Mediterranean, Casablanca, North Africa, Sicily, Italy and southern France. During the time I was gone I faithfully sent my five dollars a year to pay for my lot on South Beach Annex, for a total of $50.

It wasn't until after I completed my naval service and college that I returned to the Northwest. My job at Boeing Flight Test gave me weekends off to once more enjoy Beckett Point.

With this weekend time off we spent time at my Dad's cabin, worked on its upkeep and spent time fishing. Without facilities, we could not spend overnight time at our South Beach Annex lot. When a free 100-year old cabin that was 8' x 12' became available during a motel remodel in Port Townsend we took advantage of the opportunity and had the cabin transported by truck to our lot on the beach. This move gave us a kitchen, dining area and a bathroom. We used our camping tent for a bedroom. Our septic system was typical for the time. Water and power was available from Club sources.

This worked for several years until we decided we needed more permanent quarters. We designed an addition to add on the beach side of our old 8'x12' cabin and its dimensions were 18'x20'. A "bill of materials", (a list of lumber from the new drawings) was made and we headed out into the woods where a gypo saw mill was sawing up wood. This mill was in the deep woods, 100' trees all around. The owner of the mill accepted our list of materials and said come back in a few days. We were asking for hemlock heavy beams, cedar 2½"x4½"s and 1"x12" cedar siding in 8' plus lengths. An additional list of materials was made for finished lumber products, such as cedar 2"x4"s for a 24' laminated and 4'x8' plywood for roofing.

Footings were dug, concrete poured, and the building was on its way. The saw mill completed its job and we trailered the wood from the forest to the Point. Surprisingly enough cedar wood was readily available. Labor was from family members and relatives, mostly Grandpa and Grandma Mc Ilroy. Construction was pretty typical, the main deck was fabricated and when finished the framing was done on the deck and sides raised as they were finished. Four cloister windows were on each side and the front had four 6"x3" windows.

After pricing the glass for the windows, we soon headed for the junk yards in Seattle for second hand window glass. Plate glass from the third story of a demolished Seattle building was found. There were no large sheets of used glass available so the bay side was reframed for the two 3'x3' glass windows instead of 6' panels.

The main ceiling beam, 4'x16'x24', was laminated with glue and fasteners. An end to end camber was built in to insure a level beam when installed and leveled. It turned out perfect when installed and loaded. The rough siding installed was 1"x12"x10' cedar planks covered with building paper and finished by 1"x8" tapered cedar siding. When finished, we were very pleased, it all tuned out very well. We had a cutout for a fireplace, but this was left for a later time.

We were pleased with the addition for many years. However upon retirement the urge to redo the old motel cabin and need for a septic system update started us working on a further update. Times were different now, clearance from the Club, county engineers and the county Health Department was required before anything could be done. The Club quickly approved our plans, the County Engineer tested us ….. when reviewing our plans until one day he said, "Oh are you just building 'a cabin'?" The final obstacle with the County Engineer was with the 4"x16"x24' beams we planned to fabricate by lamination. He said the state no longer allowed that type of construction even though we explained we had one installed for over 15 years with no problems. The answer was no ….. so we redesigned the beam using two 2"x12"x24' planks with a ½" plywood center capped by a 2"x4" plank top and bottom.. This assembly was glued and fastened into a beam assembly with the side scored in 1"x¾" pattern so that it appeared to be a laminated type beam. Our drawings and permit were then signed off.

Then we were okay with the county, but now the Health Department lost our plans for a number of months but when found this was soon okay and we were ready to build. The framing and overall construction was typical with the exception of the tear down of the old motel cabin. It contained our kitchen and bathroom. We needed those two items until the new ones were done. What we did was to build the new addition around the old section, removing the roof as the new roof was installed. When the new kitchen and bathroom were completed there was about a two hour interval between the change from old to new. The old kitchen and bathroom were removed via the back door. All remaining parts of the old motel cabin went the same way. The cabin was soon complete and we were lucky to find siding similar to the old cabin siding, so the overall addition looked perfect. Our permits were signed off and our new septic system with new design sand mound was also complete.

Our final chore was to fill the blank space in the north wall with a fireplace. You start with a lot of books, make a lot of measurements, learn about fire brick, finish brick, lentals, inserts and "mud". Virginia and Marianne came thru with a terrific mud mix and finish work that made our fireplace perfect. It was a total family effort and ended with a great job, well done.

As a family we worked hard together and now we are thoroughly enjoying the fruits of our efforts, year in and year out.

Fred Mc Ilroy
1130 Beckett Point Rd.

First addition to 8x12 motel cabin

Final addition under construction

COOK'S SMOKE HOUSE

I am pretty sure when Sam built his smoke house at Beckett Point to smoke some of his salmon catch, he had no idea what would follow. To look ahead it would become a community smoke house for a time.

It was after the late 1950's and there were lots of salmon around to be at the Point was my Dad's place up on the hill above Swede's Row with the tall trees around and Diamond Point and Protection Island on the horizon. It was a great place for vacation days.

With all the salmon around people were "limiting" which meant salmon to fry, bake or BBQ and salmon to can and salmon to salt down in kegs with rock salt. But with all that there were still more salmon to take care of. Sam with his new smoke house did not have any problem. His extra salmon went in to be smoked and it came out a golden dark brown and the fish would just come off in flakes. Well, after some of this smoked fish showed up at Beckett Point pot-lucks and picnic tables, taste buds watered at the thought.

I don't know who was the first to ask Sam if they could hang a fish or two in the shack, but once it started there were more requests. Soon there was more fish than room and 2-1/2 days of a weekend could not handle it all. There were a few people living at the Point by now and they gave a hand at maintaining the burning and smoking embers that smoked and slow cooked the fish. The smoked fish was such a huge success that it was soon a full week to week operation. There may have been some gaps but not many, when salmon was available. Now here is how we participated. We vacationed on weekends often at Beckett and you could always count when a light showed at Dad's cabin the next morning someone would swing by and get us scheduled in to the smoking routine. They loved it when we stayed a week or more. Fun at the time and fond memories now. I feel the taste buds stirring.

Fred Mc Ilroy — 1130 Beckett Point Road

OUT OF THE SKY

It was Labor Day and the end of a three-day weekend at Bali Hal Beckett Point. After lunch we were beginning to pack up for the trip home. We were starting to clean the boats out prior to putting them away. We hadn't noticed that the fog was rallying in from the west and the cloud ceiling was lowering until a yellow propeller-driven plane a 1957 Beaver came in low over the cabin and headed down the bay flying low over the water.

It soon had to turn around and head back because of a low overcast of clouds. Now as we watched the aircraft return we noticed the fog covering the Point behind us and across the bay to Diamond Point. The pilot now seeing the area as "socked in" zoomed over the cabin into the fog and immediately turned 180 degrees. He came back out of the fog and was now forced by the conditions to land on the Bay.

By this time we were all standing on the beach watching these events unfold. The airplane made a smooth landing and the pilot taxied up to our beach area and with great skill turned, cut the engine and drifted tail first back into the beach.

The door of the aircraft opened. The pilot climbed down on the pontoon and took his shoes and socks off. He slipped gingerly into the cold water and checked around the pontoons to insure they were not being damaged. As the pilot checked around a passenger climbed out and down to the float. The pilot without saying too much backed up to the float the passenger climbs on his back and the pilot carried him ashore. We could see this person was over six feet tall, an elderly gentleman, who immediately pulls out a pack of smokes and lights one up. (We found out later this person was 92 years old and on his 39th fishing trip to the Canadian waters north of us.). The pilot continued to unload passengers until there were four on the beach and he was the fifth. There were two women and two men passengers.

The pilot said he must fly VFR (visual flying rules), therefore when the weather closed in on him he had no choice but to land. After considering his options, which were nil, he accepted our advice to tie up to our buoy. One lady mentioned she could use a bathroom, so Fred IV immediately asked the entire group down to our cabin looking to me for permission which was given.

The group moved into our cabin greeting Virginia, Molly, Vern, Marianne, Ruthie, Sam, Adam and Fred III. George, Freddie and I had already met them on the beach. Meanwhile, the pilot skillfully tied the airplane to the buoy and made it secure. Fred IV and George took the Harbor Craft with the motor out to pick the pilot up and returned him to the shore. Now on the beach, he used his cell phone to contact Sound Flight, his home office at Renton Field. At this time they were of no help as they did not have any information on our area weather conditions. Vern used his CB radio in his car for weather and the pilot used the airplane radio for the same when Freddie took him out to the plane, but there was no good news. Now they had to wait for the weather to clear.

They were an interesting group of people. The pilot had been flying planes for many years, most recently in Alaska, California, British Columbia, and now in our area. One couple was from Long Island, New York, and the husband shows us his business card. He was a hunting guide registered in New York State and did his guiding on Long Island. His wife was in the medical field and held about 50 shows all around the U.S. each year. The guide had a great sense of humor and caught Vern, Fred III and I, as we were standing out in front of the cabin, all off guard when he asked us if we would like to see him talk to a flock of ducks floating in the water about 300 feet offshore. We assured him we would like to see him do this. He then cupped his hands around his mouth like a megaphone and shouted in a loud voice, "Hey ducks!" Of course we expected something else, but such a dry sense of humor gave us all a chuckle.

While the above was taking place outside the cabin, inside the cabin Marianne, Virginia, Ruthie, Molly, Sam and Adam were feeding the guests baked potatoes with all the trimmings leftover from lunch and supplemented by brownies baked by Ruthie. They also found out inside the house the man who had lit the smokes on the beach was from San Diego, California, was 92 years old, was in the wholesale houseplant business and had over 300 green houses. This was his 39th trip to go fishing in northern waters. He was a real talker and between words he was lighting up and smoking. Somehow between his wit and stories the ladies, perhaps Marianne labeled him with the nickname Shady. Weird as it was maybe, we found out later he lives on Shady Lane in San Diego.

While the passengers were inside having lunch, the pilot was having a chat about the area with Vern and Fred III. The fog continued to roll in and we stopped preparation to go home. There was some doubt about the group leaving as the weather continued to get worse with thicker fog. The pilot continued to try for a weather briefing by cell phone and radio. To our surprise in about an hour the fog started lifting and the pilot thought he had a chance to go back to Seattle. The plane was swinging on the buoy so the four passengers with the pilot climbed into the Harbor Craft and with George and Fred IV in charge, they gingerly rowed out to the airplane. With all aboard, the pilot started the engine and taxied out around the Point out of our sight with the idea of taking off to the north. Once more we started packing to head for home.

To our surprise, about twenty minutes later, here comes the plane back around the Point. The weather had closed in again with zero ceiling. Once more the plane taxied up and tied up to the buoy. We put the Harbor Craft back in the water. Fred and George ferried the group back up to the beach. The pilot was disappointed but the passengers said he was the boss and they trusted him to make all the right decisions. There was some discussion among the flying group about what to do. The pilot did not want to leave his plane as the passengers thought about going into Port Townsend.

Well, believe it or not, once more the weather started to lift again. Fred and George ferried the five people back out to the airplane. There wasn't much freeboard, but they sat quite still and they were careful leaving the boat when boarding the airplane. Once more the plane engine started and the plane disappeared around the Point not to return. Once more we put the boat away, packed and left for home.

We had a nice letter from the New York couple who were very impressed with Fred, George, Ruthie, Sam and Adam. It was great to see such a nice family of children. From Shady at Christmas came candy for the kids, canned salmon for all of us, a nice card and story about how many tuna he had just caught. The lady from Seattle, a Law Assistant and a fisherwoman, gave us a nice salmon which we all enjoyed.

Sound Flight came through the best though a free two hour flight around Puget Sound for all the kids, Vein and Fred III for the things they did. All in all, a great adventure.

Now two framed letters grace the walls of the cabin, one from New York and one from San Diego, that with glowing terms describe what nice kids we have in our family. These from strangers who saw these children for only a few hours.

Beckett Point Summer Resident Whale

It was the summer of 1996 when a Gray Whale made Discovery Bay its daily feeding ground. It was a real surprise to the Mc Ilroys and Van Divers to see a whale show up in their Beckett Point front yard (Discovery Bay) and spend part of the summer feeding there. Most days the whale would enter the Bay on the Diamond Point side; move into the area in a slow porposing routine, apparently bottom feeding. He would continue into the Bay for some distance and make a turn that would bring him back out of the Bay passing close inshore to Beckett Point.

We would see the Whale's head break water, then came a spout of water and stale air as it exhaled its breath, the back would show and finally the tail breaking water and going perpendicular to the water surface and then slide down into the water.

A beautiful routine and sight to see. We made it a point to stay clear but, one day Fred Mc Ilroy IV and George Van Diver were fishing when the whale passed close aboard to their boat. The photo shows the close encounter. We did enjoy the visit that summer

Fred W. Mc Ilroy
1130 Beckett Point Rd.

New Jersey Girl Wins Beckett Point Fishing Derby

I, Fred Mc Ilroy II moved back to the NW when college was finished in February 1954. The NW was all new to wife Virginia. She took to the NW fairly well and enjoyed our outings to Beckett Point where we stayed at Fred Mc Ilroy Sr.'s cabin as our cabin had not been built on the South Beach Annex. Virginia had not been an outdoors person in the East, but took to the NW life in good spirits. She took part in everything that came along, so when it was Beckett Point Derby time in September she jumped right in.

Our rig was a skiff and a ten horse motor.

The early morning excitement of signing for the Derby, jostling around fishermen, boats, and motors set the stage for the day.

It was about 6:00 am, the sun was up, it was preparing to be a perfect day. There was no wind, so the water was calm, and the temperature felt great. All in all, all we needed was fish. Virginia had a pretty standard fishing pole and reel and she had checked herself out on the equipment the day before. Her fishing rig was a Mahon flasher and a fresh herring with the hooks buried and tied in. With the rig over the side in the water the movement looked great. The run we chose was between Cape George and Beckett Point. There were no hits in our first three runs. It was in our fourth run about 9:00 am that excitement started in our boat. Virginia's line had started reeling out with a high pitch whine. Virginia grabs the pole, restrains the line and sets the hook. Virginia had fun and thrills for about 15 minutes while the fish broke water several times. As an amateur at Salmon fishing she did great as she attempted to bring the fish in. When finally alongside the boat to her the fish appeared to be a real monster. Her fish was boated and we headed for the ramp for weigh in. The weight came in as 15 lbs and 7 ounces. We headed back out, but caught no more fish inside the Derby time limit.

Virginia's fish was the top for the day for the Women and she felt good about wining and the NW.

Fred W. Mc Ilroy
1130 Beckett Point Rd.

Christmas Drink

Christmas time is a time to be at home, but this year was to be a different time at our parents in Port Townsend. It was a wonderful time of presents, great gobs of food and many friends and relatives to be with and enjoy.

After an early Christmas dinner where food and drink was plentiful, my dad, Fred W. Mc Ilroy, Sr., called me aside and said lets go for a ride. It was just he and I, and it was soon apparent we were headed for Beckett Point. We soon stopped at one of the first cabins at the bottom of the hill. It was Charley Seely's home. My dad hadn't said anything about what we were doing here, but I was soon to find out Charlie was in the front room of his home. Out the front window you could see the Bay, Diamond Point Protection Island and Cape George. Charley was facing this view as we came in, and as if our arrival was a signal the street door opened seven more times, each time a person joined the semi-circle facing the bay.

There were now nine of us facing the view, there had been nods of recognition and short words spoken. Apparently the group was complete and like magic a fifth of bourbon appeared in Charlie's hands and the cap had been removed. As I looked around I saw familiar faces, Beckett Point faces, ones that were always there when something needed to be done for the Point. I began to see a bond between these men that was way above the average. I was starting to see now that a nod of the head was a thousand-words expressed in an instant. Charlie had now taken a drink out of the bottle of bourbon and was passing it on to his neighbor. Short stories were told by various members of the group, such as comments on Lyle's big fish of the year, as the bottle traveled down the line and back. It seems it was a review of the past year at Beckett Point and the good things that happened there. These men were good friends and enjoyed being with each other. I think most of the stories I heard were true …. could they have been shaded a little …. I don't know, but I doubt it. These guys knowing each other so well did not have to embellish theft tales to impress each other.

My sips from the bottle were small, but the bottle soon emptied and was set aside. The room was emptied as it had silently filled. We too departed, me puzzling over what had transpired and knowing that discussing the event with my Dad was unnecessary. I mostly thought about these men from different walks of life, who pulled together in efforts for Beckett Point.

Fred W. Mc Ilroy

During World War II we had as many as six soldiers staying in our cabin as they were manning a search light that was in a building a few lots from us towards North Beach. I was only 8 or 9 at the time but remember going out to Beckett and visiting with them. My father had served in France during World War I and I think he wanted to help during World War II also. I know he was an air raid warden in Port Townsend during that time. Once I was out in a row boat and went too far so some of the soldiers came and retrieved me. In the 1940's, not sure of exact date, a lady driving down the hill did not make the curve and ended in the lagoon.

When the tide used to come under the road in the South Beach areas the water would come right up to the road where the playground is now across from our cabin and Anne Plut Woods and I would sit on one of the many logs that were there and fish for little crabs and bullheads. There was a dock out in front of Gil Thomas's about where Bill Smith lives now and we could tie up boats, fish from it, etc. This was in the 40's. We would also take logs from the beach and sit on them and row around the area.

During the late 1920's and 30's a group of men, including my father Edward (Ted) Drake, stayed in a cabin on the beach at Cape George and went fishing from there. In those days the fishing was fantastic. The use of outboard motors was frowned upon and everyone had his own skiff to row around the area. To get to the beach at Cape George the men had to drive through the farmer owner's pasture, opening and closing several gates. One day someone left a gate open and some of the cattle got out. The farmer was very annoyed and restricted access to the beach. That was when the group of men decided to look for another location and settled on Beckett Point. They formed the corporation of Cape George Fishermen and surveyed the area for lots. Each member of the corporation could lease one lot per person, two per family. The price per lease was $50. My dad built one of the first cabins on the point about 1939. The lot next to our cabin, West Beach #3 was in my mother, Winifred Drake's name. There were no facilities, water, sewer, electricity, etc. Water had to be carried from town and we had commercial toilets and kerosene lamps and candles.

The water around Beckett used to be full of commercial fishing boats and they would sometimes give us a salmon.

Diane Lux
West Beach #2

Drake/Lux cabin before fire spring 2009

The new Drake/Lux cabin as it looks today

During the 1982 filming of Officer and Gentleman in the Port Townsend area the Lux cabin became a frequent get-away spot for cast members to travel to and hang out at. Mike Lux has made note that with the cast different egocentricities, it was an interesting time.

RINGING OF THE BELL

Cabin of Roy & Geraldine Craig

Roy installed a 10 inch brass bell on the flagpole above the bulkhead. His stated purpose was to use it to summon kids in from fishing in front of the cabin, however we believed it to be more of a way to notify everyone it was "5 O' Clock Somewhere." The night after installation, everyone being tucked in, neighbors several cabins to the West came along the bulkhead and attached a fish line to the lanyard. They then started ringing the bell, quit, and rang it again. The third time Roy got up and went out on the porch he cut loose exclaiming what he thought about the pranksters. After this the bell ringers cut the line at the lanyard and retreated, all then was quiet. The next day Roy discovered the fish line remnant but nobody ever owned up to the deed. It was kept a secret for some 20 years until during a 2000 New Year's Eve party, loose lips let the story out.

Neil & Rosalynn (Craig) Gallagher
South Beach Annex #4 & 5

PHOTOS HELD IN TIME

When we decided to renovate the kitchen in December, 2008 we pulled out the old cabinets, and under the corner cabinet I found an old photo of Mr. Sensabaugh, previous leaseholder. In the background of the old photo, there were some old sailing ships.

So, I found a photo of Klaus with sailing ships in the picture and just before everything was sealed up I put both photos back under the cabinet to be found sometime in the future, probably in another 20 years.

Klaus & Marilyn Butz
Highway Heights #10 & 11

NEW YEAR'S EVE PARTY 1999/2000

For the Millennium celebration Rosalynn and Neil hosted a New Year's Eve party at their cabin at Beckett. Motel rooms were booked in Port Townsend for out of area guests. Motor homes and campers utilized the turn around and over nighters filled our cabin. All Beckett Point was invited and many attended. The garage was cleared out, heaters brought in, table and chairs put up. Everyone participated in helping with food and refreshments and the party was on.

We had a fireworks display at midnight and a large number of flares were lit and floated into the bay.

Captain Robert Burns entertained with stories of his years as a Foss tugboat skipper delivering supplies to the remote Native villages and Military installations on the Arctic shores of Northern Alaska. He told of his experience, being awakened early December 7, 1941 in his barracks outside Honolulu, hearing planes overhead. He witnessed the Japanese attack on Pearl Harbor and the destruction of the U.S. Pacific Fleet. He told of his Pacific enlistment duties throughout the War, and it was most interesting to hear his stories.

Dick Easter told of his University of Washington crew member days prior to World War II and the competitions held in Berlin 1939. He talked of his long term employment with Merrill Lynch after the war. He started as a delivery boy with the San Francisco office and progressed up through the ranks.

Alice Murray told of her secretarial days with the Inland Boatman's Union and her social connections in Olympia. I had always tried to get Alice to spill about the old days of Olympia politics but true to her "zipped lip" convictions she would never reveal much other than a wink or two and a (Oh, Neil, you don't want to know).

After assurances the statutes of limitations had expired a confession was given concerning the loud boom out on the water many years previously. Some years past on a 4th of July night, after the celebration and everyone had retired, a float device was rigged up upon which a box of powder (stump dynamite) and a timer detonator were floated out into the bay. When it went off, Beckett Point "rocked." Although through the years, fingers were pointed nobody admitted to the deed/until the party.

One attending out of town guest was a very dear doctor friend of ours from Puyallup. He was also a participant in the traditional Polar Bear Club. Throughout the evening he had chided me that after midnight it was his intention to take his "dip." I hadn't taken him seriously but sure enough a little after midnight he entertained by taking his swim however he forgot to mention that he was doing such au natural except for his shoes. After a real dressing down by his wife we got him redressed and placed by the stove.

Shortly after, I was called out to the garage. It seems one of our other Puyallup guests had taken offense to a Beckett Point guest who while dancing had inappropriately used his hands on his dance partners behind. The dance partner being wife of the Puyallup guest. Nothing serious happened but I was told the next day that my statement of "you gotta do what you gotta do" had not helped diffuse things.

The party wound down and after some clean up I headed to bed. About daylight I awoke and heard voices downstairs. Upon investigating I found Mr. Easter and our daughter number 2 engaged in an intense cribbage game. It was quite a party and I am glad we had ushered in the new century amongst so many nice people and friends

It was however with great sadness that some 4 months later Dr. Ron was diagnosed with brain cancer and succumbed some months later. His illness was of short duration and our family misses him and his antics. During the following decade Cap, Dick and Alice left us but certainly Beckett Point is a more interesting place from their time here.

Neil & Rosalynn Gallagher
South Beach Annex #4 & 5

Beckett Point photo (Circa late 1940's/before over tide of 1951. The large deposit of logs post 1951 in lagoon area are not shown). House on the far right showing the chimney, South Beach Annex #4, built late 1940's.

NOTE: Dock and piling with boat near mid South Beach.
Courtesy by Mike and Sue Stevens, South Beach #13 and #14

Late 1970's — Long time Beckett Point residents Ivan Barnett South Beach Annex #10, Minnie Hughes South Beach Annex #11

During the mid 1990's the *Port Townsend Leader* made note of a film being made using sites on the Olympic Peninsula. Primarily the film was being shot in Forks, however the unique construction of Burke's West Beach #8 cabin drew their attention and was incorporated into the film. At that time the film was unnamed but the Leader noted it was the story of a "logger on the downhill slide to degradation," Hmmm. Whether it was ever released or not is unknown at this writing.

It's "5 O' Clock Somewhere" – Jack Meyer, Larry & Betsy Lee

50's/Swain family - Cliff, Bea, Glenda (Cable), Becky and guest

CAPE GEORGE FISHERMEN, Inc.
BECKETT POINT
PORT TOWNSEND, WASHINGTON

This Is to Certify That

Nick D'Andrea & Jennie D'Andrea

Is a Member in Good Standing with Dues Paid to

Dec. 31, 1980   Deane A. Lux, Secretary

We also have winter

Summer on the beach

Let's walk the dog

Whoops!!!!

Beckett Point early on known as Fort Point.

(From official records/Miller and Going/Civil Engineers 189

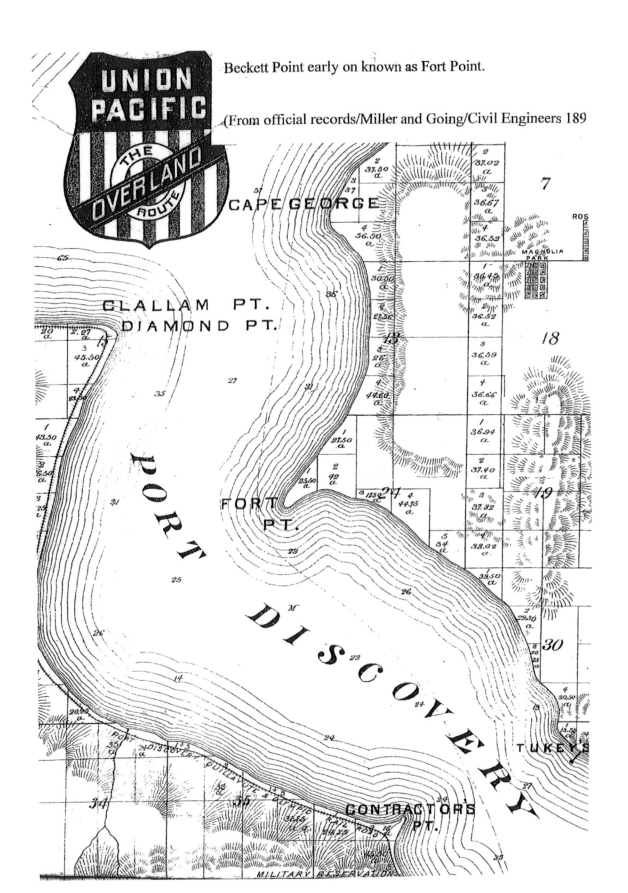

87740

ARTICLES OF INCORPORATION OF

CAPE GEORGE FISHERMEN, INCORPORATED

KNOW ALL MEN BY THESE PRESENTS:

That the undersigned, N. W. Raynor, Roy Dale, H. L. Hirtzler, Lyall L. Aray and Cecil Guptill, each being of full age and a citizen of the United States, have associated themselves together for the purpose of forming a corporation under the provisions of Sections 3868 to 3900 inclusive, Remington's Revised Statutes of Washington, and in pursuance thereof do hereby sign and acknowledge the following Articles of Incorporation in triplicate, and do state as follows:

I.

That the corporate name of this corporation shall be "CAPE GEORGE FISHERMEN, INCORPORATED."

II.

That the purposes for which this corporation is formed are the following:

1. To provide a recreational area for members of the corporation.

2. To promote and stimulate interest in salt water fishing, and provide for competition.

3. To promote, by precept and example, the highest standards of sportsmanship

4. To aid in the dissemination of information touching upon the propogation and preservation of game, game fish, and food fish.

5. To assist in the observance and enforcement of our game laws.

6. To purchase, lease from others, and otherwise acquire, sell, convey, transfer, lease to others, and otherwise dispose of, mortgage, or otherwise encumber real or personal property.

That the corporation shall have the capacity to act possessed by a natural person. But this corporation shall have authority to perform only such actions as are necessary and proper to accomplish its purposes and which are not repugnant to law.

III.

That the location and Post-Office address of this corporation shall be the City of Port Townsend, Jefferson County, Washington.

IV.

That the term for which this corporation shall exist is fifty years from and after its incorporation.

V.

That the number of trustees shall be seven, and the names of the trustees who shall manage the affairs of the corporation for the first six months are:

Name	Residence
N. W. Raynor	Port Townsend, Washington
Roy Dale	Port Townsend, Washington
H. L. Hirtzler	Port Townsend, Washington
Bert Carr	Port Townsend, Washington
Bruce Blevins	Port Townsend, Washington
S. L. Lockhart	Port Townsend, Washington
Cecil Guptill	Port Townsend, Washington

In Witness Whereof, we have hereunto set our hands in triplicate this 27th day of June, 1939.

STATE OF WASHINGTON)
) SS
COUNTY OF JEFFERSON)

    This is to certify that on the 27th day of June, 1939, there appeared personally before me, H. W. Raynor, Roy Dale, H. L. Hirtzler, Lyall L. Arey, and Cecil Guptill, to me known to be the persons described in and who executed the foregoing Articles of Incorporation, and they, and each of them, did acknowledge and declare to me that he executed the same freely and voluntarily, for the uses and purposes therein mentioned.

    IN WITNESS WHEREOF, I have hereunto set my hand and official seal in triplicate the day and year first above written.

                                                 W. J. Daley
                                           Notary Public in and for the State of Washington, residing at Port Townsend.

South Beach Annex 1A, 1
1220 Beckett Point Road
Steve and Rebecca Hanson

1950 – Carl Craig
1959 – Cliff Swain
2001 – Glenda (Swain) Cable
2016 – Steve Hanson

South Beach Annex 2
Lot
Steve Hanson

No photo

1941 – Mrs. Hansen
1950 – Stella Craig
1959 – Bea Swain
2001 – Richard Cable
2016 – Steve Hanson

South Beach Annex 3
1210 Beckett Point Road
Portia Mather-Hempler, Jim Hempler

1945 – Chester Irle
1951 – Rev. Lester Mather

South Beach Annex 4, 5
1200 Beckett Point Road
Neil and Rosalyn Gallagher

1947 – Edna Hill
1967 – Geraldine Craig
1994 – Rosalynn Gallagher

1945 – Tom Baker
1947 – Dan Hill
1967 – Roy Craig
1994 – Neil Gallagher

South Beach Annex 6
1198 Beckett Point Road
Michael Millikan

No Photo

1946 – Charles Smith
1970 – Brad Kenyon
1977 – Janet Schenk
2016 – Michael Millikan

South Beach Annex 7
1196 Beckett Point Road
Shane Cline

No Photo

1945 – Mrs. Bert Carr
1946 – Ira Carr
1956 – Jeannette Smith
1970 – Louretta Kenyon
1977 – Leon Schenk
2016 – Shane Cline

South Beach Annex 8, 9
1190 Beckett Point Road
Dennis Ankeny

1945 – Mrs. Del Wollam
1954 – Dioma Sweitzer
1992 – Dennis Ankeny

South Beach Annex 10
1180 Beckett Point Road
Carol Jinks

1945 – Herb Swanson
1952 – Ivan Barnett
1987 – Loretta Wheeler
1993 – Clint Hattrup
2000 – Daniel Speth
2016 – Carol Jinks

South Beach Annex 11
1170 Beckett Point Road
Don and Michelle Porth

1946 – Earl Tonning
1960 – Bill Howard
1969 – Minnie Hughes
1982 – Dorothy Hughes
2006 – Jerry Hutter
2009 – Don Porth

South Beach Annex 12
1160 Beckett Point Road
Karl Erickson

1947 – Harry Gauthier
2003 – Karl Erickson

South Beach Annex 13
1154 Beckett Point Road
Gerald and Melanie Gauthier

No photo

1947 – Harry Gauthier
1982 – Gerald Gauthier
2012 – Melanie Gauthier

South Beach Annex 14
1150 Beckett Point Road
Lonny Kvinsland

1945 – Della Zieke
1956 – Homer Hughes
1971 – Mary Kvinsland
1978 – Lonnie Kvinsland

South Beach Annex 15, 16
1140 Beckett Point Road
Debbie Kennedy and Chris Meyer

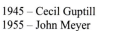

1945 – Harry Campbell
1954 – Lawrence Stenstrom
1959 – Lorraine Meyer
2016 – Debbie Meyer Kennedy

1945 – Cecil Guptill
1955 – John Meyer
2016 – Chris Meyer

South Beach Annex 17
1130 Beckett Point Road
Marianne VanDiver

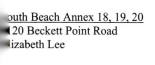

1942 – Marie Mc Ilroy
1945 – Fred Mc Ilroy Jr.
2016 – Marianne VanDiver

South Beach Annex 18, 19, 20
1120 Beckett Point Road
Elizabeth Lee

1945 – Andrew Mc Ilroy
1976 – Virginia Mc Ilory
2013 – Elizabeth Lee

1939 – Clare Bunge
1946 – Mrs. Leo Ziel
1975 – Elizabeth Lee

1945 – Clara Bill
1946 – Leo Ziel
1970 – Beverly Munter
1975 – Dick McCurdy
1979 – Larry Lee
2019 – Elizabeth Lee

<u>South Beach Annex 21</u>
110 Beckett Point Road
Michelle Brooks

1948 – Walter Jones
1952 – F. Ziel
1971 – Eleanor McCurdy
1989 – James Grabicki
2000 – John Brooks
2009 – Michelle Brooks

<u>South Beach Annex 22, 23</u>
1100 Beckett Point Road
Clyde amd Colleen McQueen

1945 – William Campbell
1978 – Harvey Moliter
1980 – Jean Kinney
2001 – Clyde McQueen

1978 – Harry Militer
1980 – Gary Kinney
2001 – Clyde McQueen

<u>South Beach Annex 24, 25</u>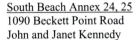
1090 Beckett Point Road
John and Janet Kennedy

1945 – George Cotton
1953 – Ethel Lewis
1985 – Janet Kennedy

1946 – Harold Lewis
1985 – John Kennedy Estate

<u>South Beach Annex 26, 27</u>
1080 Beckett Point Road
Ed and Rosemarie Edwards

1945 – Nora Tjemsland
1955 – Ruth Wolfe
1958 – Frank Robinson
1962 – Annamae Matson
1999 – Rosemarie Edwards

1945 – Ole Tjemsland
1952 – Kristine Margrath
1961 – Dr. Tom Matson
1999 – Edward Edwards

<u>South Beach Annex 28</u>
1070 Beckett Point Road
Mark Hawley

1945 – N. Lewthwaite
1951 – Chester Gillette
1976 – Ed & Josephine Hawley
2002 – Mark Hawley

<u>South Beach Annex 29</u>
1064 Beckett Point Road
Vanessa Gemmill

No Photo

1945 – R. Osborn
1958 – Bill Shinkle
1974 – Richard Gemberling
2004 – Vernon Barnett

<u>South Beach Annex 30</u>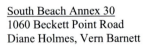
1060 Beckett Point Road
Diane Holmes, Vern Barnett

1945 – Joe Buchillo
1955 – N. Roll
1958 – Lillian Shinkle
1974 – Richard Gemberling
2004 – Vernon Barnett

South Beach Annex 31
1050 Beckett Point Road
Yvonne Monroe

1947 – Ralph Cross
1958 – Joe Owens
1967 – Russell Brain
1974 – Yvonne (Brain) Monroe

South Beach Annex 32
1040 Beckett Point Road
Ruth Short Estate

1945 – David Hopkins
1950 – E. Hinkley
1959 – Lawrence Short
1975 – Ruth Short

South Beach Annex 33, 34
1030 Beckett Point Road
Jim and Susan Bumgarner

1945 – George Baxter
1952 – Clarence Easton
1961 – Marjorie Hendricks
1978 – Susan Bumgarner
2013 – Jim Bumgarner

1946 – Lester Bumgarner
1952 – Ralph Hendricks
1978 – Susan Bumgarner

South Beach Annex 35
Lot
Kevin O'Leary

No Photo

1950 – Milo Silva
1955 – Fred Foster
2005 – Evan Hall
2008 – Kevin O'Leary

South Beach Annex 36
Lot
Club Property

1948 – Raymond Goodrich
1959 – N. Roll
1971 – Gary Ruggles
2007 – Rena Behar
2019 – Club Property

South Beach Annex 37, 38
1020 Beckett Point Road
Ron and Susan Henry

1946 – Bert Lashua
1953 – Robert Growder
1969 – Jean DeLoe
1973 – Linda Allen
1998 – Steven Enge
2014 – Ron Henry

1949 – Jesse Lashua
1953 – Harriett Growder
1973 – Charles Allen
1998 – Kathy Pool
2014 – Susan Henry

South Beach Annex 39, 40
Lot
D. Freelove

No Photo

1949 – Alma Swanson
1950 – Romay Brandenberg
1996 – Almeta Peterson/Gene Roberts
2001 – JD & Jean Freelove

South Beach Annex 41
Lot
Chris D'Andrea

No Photo

1948 – Myra Thomas
1962 – Nicholas D'Andrea
1971 – Jean D'Andrea
2011 – Chris D'Andrea

South Beach 1, 2
870 Beckett Point Road
Karel Reeves

1943 – N. Lewthwaite
1944 – W. Rideout
1953 – Vivian LaVera
1977 – Karel Reeves

1940 – N. Lewthwaite
1947 – Jesse LaVera
1977 – Jerry Reeves

South Beach 3
880 Beckett Point Road
Lori Burton

1954 – John Hearing
1976 – John England
1988 – Susan Meyers
2006 – Mike DeRousie
2014 – Lori Burton

South Beach 4, 5
890 Beckett Point Road
William and Patti Sahlinger

1940 – John Geddes
1977 – Meril Martin
1994 – Bill Sahlinger

1940 – Thomas Gedde
1976 – Dorthy Martin
1994 – Patti Sahlinger

South Beach 6
Lot
Helen Marriott

No Photo

1940 – John Hearing
1943 – Charles Smith
1954 – Mr. H. Plut
1988 – Helen Marriott

South Beach 7
910 Beckett Point Road
Margaret Palo

1940 – Harry Plut
1988 – Thomas Plut
1995 – Margaret Palo

South Beach 8
920 Beckett Point Road
James Hradec

1942 – William Berg
1949 – John McIntyre
1965 – Helen Plut
1978 – Carol Keogh
2012 – Barbara Rosati
2016 – James Hradec

South Beach 9
930 Beckett Point Road
Barbara Blowers

1943 – John Zaccardo
1971 – Barbara Blowers
1990 – Phyllis Anderson
2005 – Barbara Blowers

South Beach 10, 11
1940 Beckett Point Road
Judy Smith

1939 – M. Gofoth
1981 – James Hansen
1990 – Rhoda Altom
1996 – Judith Smith

1964 – Cecil Clark
1966 – Harry Craig
1981 – Lavola Hansen
1990 – Robert Carlson
1996 – Bill Smith

South Beach 12
1950 Beckett Point Road
Barb Vittitoe

1940 – Ralph Camfield
1955 – Roy Doninger
1957 – Harry Cotton
1969 – Thomas Wagner
1978 – Charles Berg
1994 – Dan Berg
2019 – Barb Vittitoe

South Beach 13, 14
1960 Beckett Point Road
Mike and Sue Stevens

1940 – Gil Thomas
1961 – Roy Grobe
2004 – Mike & Sue Stevens

South Beach 15, 16
1970 Beckett Point Road
Keith and Cynthia Hansen

1945 – Thomas Spaulding
1951 – Sam Cook
1996 – Keith Hansen

1947 – Mrs. T. Spaulding
1951 – Mae Cook (Cook Family)
1994 – Bruce Taylor
1996 – Cynthia Hansen

South Beach 17
1980 Beckett Point Road
Shelly Separavich

1945 – Early Gould
1950 – Gilvert Binsfield
1969 – Roy Bignell
1977 – Alice Murray
2012 – Shelly Separavich

South Beach 18
1990 Beckett Point Road
Mary Fredeen

1963 – Bill Gurben
1969 – Rhea Bill
1975 – Robert Burns
2009 – Burns Estate
2016 – Mary Fredeen

South Beach 19
Lot
Barbara West

No Photo

1946 – Charles Guisti
1952 – Stillman Brown
1964 – Faye Thorne
1966 – Chas Gunstone
2012 – Dana Behar
2017 – Barbara West

South Beach 20
1000 Beckett Point Road
Barbara West

1946 – Robert Brown
1951 – W.H. McCorkle
1958 – Frank Shepherd
1963 – Gilbert Condon
1979 – Joan Robinson
2010 – Peter Quinn
2016 – Susan Castelot
2017 – Barbara West

South Beach 21
1010 Beckett Point Road
Chris D'Andrea

1948 – Curtis Jones
1953 – Russell Kunz
1962 – Linda D'Andrea
1963 – Nicholas D'Andrea
2011 – D'Andrea Estate
2019 – Chris D'Andrea

West Beach 1 350 Beckett Point Road Mike DeRousie			1939 – Fred Lewis 1968 – Vivian Meyers 1974 – Don Meyers 2012 – Mike DeRousie
West Beach 2 340 Beckett Point Road Diane Lux			1940 – E. Drake 1974 – Diane Lux
West Beach 3 Lot Eileen Finnigan	No Photo		1941 – M. Strong 1951 – Winifred Drake 1976 – Ed Drake 1991 – Eileen Finnigan
West Beach 4 330 Beckett Point Road Lynn O'Dell			1941 – Rudy Strong 1951 – George Huntingford 1971 – Deleo 1987 – Wifred Wachter 1995 – Dean Mitchell 2013 – Lynn O'Dell
West Beach 5, 6 320 Beckett Point Road Larry Campbell			1945 – Kent Spaulding 1955 – W. Campbell 2013 – Larry Campbell 1947 – Francis Peterson 1952 – Thomas Spaulding 1955 – Edith Campbell
West Beach 7 Lot Aleta Erickson	No Photo		1942 – Noel Caldwell 1978 – Jerry Caldwell 2016 – Aleta Erickson
West Beach 8 310 Beckett Point Road Gene Burke			1945 – I. Larson 1969 – Gene Burke
West Beach 9 300 Beckett Point Road Janet Wallin			1943 – K. Sooy 1963 – W. Bradley 1976 – Olive Paddock 1992 – Charlie Young 1993 – William Burdick 2018 – Janet Wallin

West Beach 10
790 Beckett Point Road
Tom Camburn

1943 – Chris Geick
1959 – Harmon Harrison
1980 – Judith Smith
1996 – Kimberly Fairbanks
2014 – Tom Camburn

West Beach 11, 12
780 Beckett Point Road
Darren and Connie Ross

1945 – Al Robertson
1958 – C. Easton
1967 – Clarabelle Ross
1988 – Connie Ross
2012 – Darren Ross

West Beach 13, 14
760 Beckett Point Road
Sean Ransom

1945 – Paul Dechamplain
1952 – Francis Peterson
1959 – Ed Abnett
1977 – Larry Davis
1997 – Tom Schute/Linda Scott
2017 – Sean Ransom

1972 – Al Haddock
1977 – Sandra Davis
1997 – Tom Schute/Linda Scott
2017 – Sean Ransom

West Beach 15
750 Beckett Point Road
Katherine Johnson

1941 – P. Peterson
1969 – Vivian Holland
1985 – Katherine Johnson

West Beach 16, 17
740 Beckett Point Road
Kevin and Heidi Camfield

1945 – I. Kunkel
1952 – Hugh & Lula Zeits
1985 – Phyllis Camfield
2010 – Kevin Camfield

1945 – L. Kunkel
1952 – Hugh Zeits
1985 – Thomas Camfield
2010 – Heidi Camfield

West Beach 18
730 Beckett Point Road
Linda Schick

1942 – Arvid Pearson
1954 – Abner Ellington
1973 – Doris Kvalhien
1992 – Kvalhien Trust
2016 – Linda Schick

West Beach 19, 20
720 Beckett Point Road
Margaret Carr

1946 – Mrs. Bert Carr
1973 – Margaret Mauri
2006 – Margaret Carr

1946 – Bert Carr
1971 – Roberta Wilson
2006 – Margaret Carr

West Beach 21
710 Beckett Point Road
Jerry Hawkins

1945 – Red Simcoe
1948 – Hazel Doolen
1960 – Minnie Hughes
1962 – Dwight Lopp
1986 – Don Lopp
1999 – Jerry Hawkins

West Beach 22, 23
700 Beckett Point Road
Angela Brantley

1941 – Bert Wick
1952 – Margaret Bush
1960 – Vera Westall
1990 – Westall Trust
1994 – Paul Larson
2016 – Angela Brantley

West Beach 24, 25
690 Beckett Point Road
Steve and Nanette Aurdal

1942 – F. W. Tucker
1979 – Pat Smith
2008 – Nanette Aurdal

1945 – Mrs. F. Tucker
1976 – Dave Daniels
1986 – Bev Smith
2008 – Steve Aurdal

West Beach 26, 27
680 Beckett Point Road
Steve and Nanette Aurdal

1941 – Howard Bill
1982 – Clara Chess
1996 – Ericka Urdahl
2000 – Clara Rose
2017 – Steve Aurdal

West Beach 28, 29
670 Beckett Point Road
Wendy Offield

1942 – Tony Eronomo
1985 – W. Sahlinger
1994 – Tom Grabicki
2002 – Wendy Offield

1945 – S. Learned
1954 – Mable Eronomo
1985 – W. Sahlinger
1994 – Tom Grabicki
2002 – Wendy Offield

West Beach 30
660 Beckett Point Road
Tina Albertson

1942 – Louie Morello
1974 – Gene Morello
1995 – Arnold Whedbee
2003 – James Rosenthal
2016 – Reece Carson
2019 – Tina Albertson

West Beach 31, 32
650 Beckett Point Road
Lorraine Olsen

1949 – Betty Delgardo
1957 – Evelyn Morello
2003 – Lorraine Olsen

1957 – Joe Borello
2003 – Lorraine Olsen

West Beach 33, 34
640 Beckett Point Road
Cy Easter

1942 – Joe Morello
1948 – Mrs. Chas Seely
1977 – Thora Jones
1987 – Carol Easter
1994 – Mike Easter
2016 – Cy Easter

1946 – Charles Seeley
1977 – Curtis Jones
1987 – Dick Easter
1994 – Cy Easter

West Beach 35
630 Beckett Point Road
Jon Anderson

1944 – Dan Buchillo
1950 – Gusta Lester
1990 – Norman Baumgarner
2014 – Tricia Bumgarner
2016 – Lynn Zweber
2019 – John Anderson

West Beach 36
Lot
Pamela Darling

No Photo

1944 – Dan Buchillo
1950 – Harvey Christian
1969 – B. Brown
2006 – Dana Hamar
2016 – Pamela Darling

West Beach 37
Lot
Pamela Darling

No Photo

1947 – Dan Buchillo
1969 – Harvey Christian
1976 – Ron Priest
1987 – Gene Baumgarner
2008 – Dana Hamar
2016 – Pamela Darling

North Beach 1, 2
10 View Point Lane
Julie Averill and Cindy Bolam

1939 – Bruce Blevins
1976 – E. Stewart
1989 – Joseph Daubenberg
1996 – John Swaner
2014 – Julie Averill

1961 – Kathy Brunken
1961 – Minnie Hughes
1969 – B. Blevins
1976 – E. Stewart
1989 – James Daubenberger
1996 – John Swaner
2014 – Cindy Bolam

North Beach 3
20 View Point Lane
Gary J. Logue

1939 – Louis Olsen
1968 – Helga Loque
1994 – Gary Loque

North Beach 4
0 View Point Lane
Charles Young

1939 – Lyall Arey
1986 – Lee Arey
2008 – Charles Young

North Beach 5
0 View Point Lane
Alexander Lang

1939 – Bert Carr
1946 – Jeanette Smith
1956 – Della Zieska
1997 – Mark Carr
2005 – Alexander Lang

North Beach 6
0 View Point Lane
Caroline Myers

1939 – Gus Erickson
1963 – F. Stevens
1972 – Ed Edwards
1991 – Michael Patneaude
2014 – Caroline Myers

North Beach 7
View Point Lane
Randy Powers

1939 – Doris Delgardno
1952 – L. McDaniel
1955 – Minnie Hughes
1957 – Dave Johnson
1959 – M. Bright
1996 – Joan Powers
2013 – Randy Powers

North Beach 8
70 View Point Lane
Deborah Fouts

1939 – Axel Swanson
1971 – Charles Monson
2000 – Mark Miller
2004 – Deborah Fouts

North Beach 8A
80 View Point Lane
Ann White

1939 – Peter Norby
1957 – Carl Norby
1975 – Pat Maher
2011 – Ann White

North Beach 9
90 View Point Lane
Joy Guptill

1939 – Cecil Guptill
1969 – Ruth Guptill
1979 – Joy Guptill

North Beach 10
100 View Point Lane
Larry Schmucker

1939 – Frank Smith
1956 – Walter Copeland
1989 – Linda Krapf
1993 – James Schmertz
2006 – Deb Louis Wallace
2019 – Larry Schmucker

North Beach 11
110 View Point Lane
Katy Debernardi

1939 – Harry Gauthier
1948 – Louis Thomas
1966 – Fred Sandez
2007 – Greg Rucker
2012 – Katy Debernardi

North Beach 12
120 View Point Lane
David Myers

1939 – J. With
1969 – Carl Jacobson
1975 – David Myers

North Beach 13
130 View Point Lane
Randy Carl

1939 – N. Raynor
1957 – Chester Frisendahl
1969 – Kathy Evans
1978 – Dave Evans
2002 – Gwen Evans
2011 – Tammy Rumple
2019 – Randy Carl

North Beach 14, 15
140 View Point Lane
John and Ola Englund

1939 – Carl Jacobson Davis
1950 – Art Pelkey
1966 – Eric England
2017 – John Englund

1939 – Lee Davis
1965 – Majorie Shortley
1966 – Karin England
2017 – Ola Englund

North Beach 16, 17
150 View Point Lane
Leigh Nelson

1939 – Roy Dale
1946 – Jay Foulkner
1957 – H. Carroll
1978 – Marge Denny
2011 – Leigh Nelson

1939 – Eugene Dale
1946 – Jay Foulkner
1957 – Alice Carroll
1978 – John Denny
2011 – Leigh Nelson

North Beach 18
160 View Point Lane
Dana and Rena Behar

1961 – Leslie Hawley
1966 – Katherine Rule
1991 – Roy Waugh
2006 – Dana Behar

99

Hill Park 1A, 1, 2
554 Beckett Point Road
Kathy Acree

1951 – John Ellis
1957 – Robert Mc Ilroy
1979 – Andrew Mc Ilroy
1989 – Randi Rhode
1999 – Glen Stoody
2003 – Kathy Acree

1951 – John Ellis
1957 – Robert Mc Ilroy
1979 – Andrew Mc Ilroy
1989 – Randi Rhode
1999 – Glen Stoody
2003 – Kathy Acree

Hill Park 2A
642 Beckett Point Road
Robert Dishington

1940 – F. W. Mc Ilroy
1978 – Ralph Canfield
2002 – Karen Cartwel
2003 – Robert Dishington

Hill Park 3, 4
552 Beckett Point Road
Zachary Elan

1944 – Homer Phelps
1958 – Karl Schweitzer
1985 – Mary Holcomb
1992 – Candice Goodwin
1996 – David Evans
2013 – Zachary Elan

1947 – Homer Phelps
1959 – Ethel Schweitzer
1985 – Harry Holcomb
1992 – Charles Goodwin
1996 – David Evans
2013 – Zachary Elan

Hill Park 3A, 4A
644 Beckett Point Road
Chuck and Lila Moses

1940 – Dell Williams
1954 – Beverly Stinson
1964 – Bill Comrade
1968 – Alan Hodge
1973 – Olaf Dahl
2014 – Lila Moses

1944 – Harold Bankcroft
1954 – Dell Wollas
1954 – R. Stinson
1968 – Mary Hodge
1973 – Elaine Dahl
2014 – Chuck Moses

Hill Park 5, 6
Lot
Michael Korinek and Christine Heycke

No Photo

1944 – Ashley Bullen
1979 – Tom Morello
2003 – Lisa Aniballi
2015 – Michael Korinek

1946 – Georgia Bullen
1979 – Janet Morello
2003 – Lisa Aniballi
2015 – Christine Heycke

Hill Park 5A
Lot
Katherine Weissmann

No Photo

1959 – Gail Robinson
1982 – Verna Vitterer
1985 – Rande Gjerstad
2019 – Katherine Weissmann

Hill Park 7
Lot
Michael Korinek

No Photo

1940 – T.A. Crosby
1962 – E. Becker
1975 – Pat Simmons
1978 – Eugene Moga
2001 – Mahlon Clements
2019 – Michael Korinek

Hill Park 8, 9
494 Beckett Point Road
Mahlon Clements

1959 – Elsie Schweizter
1964 – Laverne Simmons
1978 – Greg Moga
2001 – Mahlon Clements

1940 – Ken McMillan
1958 – Schweitzer
1964 – Pat Simmons
1978 – Anna Moga
2001 – Mahlon Clements

Hill Park 10, 11, 12, 13, 14
492 Beckett Point Road
Greg Moga

1940 – A. Carr
1944 – Ralph Johnson
1949 – Stan Doolan
1959 – Gust Hendrickson
1978 – Eugene Moga
1994 – Greg Moga

1948 – Helen Tollefson
1966 – Joyce Blessinger
1996 – Greg Moga

Highway Heights 1, 1A Lot Tracy Hudson and Patrick Murphy	No Photo	1962 – Elizabeth England 1969 – Robert Perry 1976 – Mona Carbaugh 2008 – Victor Judd 2014 – Tracy Hudson	1962 – Lynn Robinson 1969 – Kathy Perry 1976 – Vernon Carbaugh 2008 – Marilyn Maloney 2014 – Patrick Murphy
Highway Heights 2A, 3A 495 Beckett Point Road Kevin and Heidi Camfield	No Photo	1962 – Darlene Hazard 1996 – M. Miller 1989 – Dan Maloney 2005 – Robert Irons 2007 – Gwen Lundgren 2014 – WF Account 2016 – Kevin Camfield	1962 – Helen Miller 1981 – Don Thompson 1989 – Karn Maloney 2005 – Robert Irons 2007 – Gwen Lundgren 2014 – WF Account 2016 – Heidi Camfield
Highway Heights 4A, 5A Club property	No Photo		
Highway Heights 6, 7 553 Beckett Point Road Sander Trust	No Photo	1945 – Nora Eikenberry 1949 – Lamoyne Sievert 1967 – Claire Barrows 1981 – Rusty Smith 1983 – Sander Trust	1945 – Gale Eikenberry 1949 – Ernest Sievert 1979 – William White 1983 – Sander Trust
Highway Heights 8, 9 555 Beckett Point Road Peter Kinney	*(photo of house)*	1943 – J. Campbell 1967 – Herbert Swasnson 2004 – Keith Hansen 2015 – Peter Kinney	1950 – C. Douglas 1956 – Orville Campbell 1967 – Herbert Swasnson 2004 – Keith Hansen 2015 – Peter Kinney
Highway Heights 10, 11, 12 557 Beckett Point Road Janet Millar	*(photo of house)*	1949 – Richard Faulkner 1958 – H. Skipley 1975 – Della Simsabaugh 2004 – Klaus Butz 2017 – Janet Mullar	1950 – E. Badger 1958 – Marion Robinson 1969 – L. Simsabaugh 2004 – Klaus Butz 2017 – Janet Mullar
Highway Heights 13, 14, 15 559 Beckett Point Road Nancy Sandberg	No Photo	1951 – Nancy Sievert 1964 – Calvin Schmidt 1974 – Robert Cook 1979 – Craig Martin 1987 – Zane Wyll 1993 – E. Dennison 1998 – J. Riordan 2004 – Karner Tretheway 2019 - Nancy Sandberg	1958 – Minnie Ness 1964 – Marilyn Schmidt 1979 – Craig Martin 1986 – Linda Ford 1993 – E. Dennison 1998 – J. Riordan 2004 – Karner Tretheway 2019 – Nancy Sandberg
Highway Heights 16 Club Property	No Photo		

Olympic View 1, 2 578 Beckett Point Road Arnold and Diana Chan	No Photo	1943 – W. Campbell 1959 – E Tulin 1983 – D. Thompson 2003 – David Green 2016 – John Green 2019 – Arnold Chan	1947 – Roger Doole 1960 – E. Tulin 1976 – F. Evans 1981 – Francis Thompson 2003 – David Green 2016 – John Green 2019 – Diana Chan
Olympic View 3, 4 576 Beckett Point Road Arnold and Diana Chan	No Photo	1939 – W. Foster 1954 – K. Loftus 1964 – J. Purdy 1985 – C. Daniels 1994 – David Green 2016 – John Green 2019 – Arnold Chan	2019 – Diana Chan
Olympic View 5 574 Beckett Point Road Robert Sudol	No Photo	1951 – W. M. Jarrett 1958 – H. Decker 1969 – Robert Anderson 1971 – L. Packa 2000 – Almeta Peterson 2016 – Robert Sudol	
Olympic View 6 572 Beckett Point Road Diane Jones	No Photo	1951 – Lawrence Zeits 1998 – Dennis Aardal 2006 – Diane Jones	
Olympic View 7, 8 Club Property	No Photo		

BECKETT POINT FISHERMENS CLUB
163 LEASEHOLD LOTS - Leaseholders of Record 06/30/19

BECKETT POINT FISHERMENS CLUB ASSESSORS PLAT RECORDED 06/24/08 #535120
Leasehold - a property held by a Lease
Ground Lease - agreement permitting use of a specific Lot

* **Lot #** - Your leased lot (left column)
* **ST #** - Street Number (right column)

SOUTH BEACH		
Lot#	Name	St#
1	REEVES, Kay	870
2	REEVES, Jer	
3	LORI BURTON	880
4	SAHLINGER, Bill	890
5	SAHLINGER, Patti	
6	MARRIOTT, Helen	
7	PALO, Margaret	910
8	HRADEC, James	920
9	BLOWERS, Barbara	930
10	SMITH, Judi	940
11	SMITH, B.	
12	VITTITOE, Barb	950
13	STEVENS, Mike	960
14	STEVENS, Sue	
15	HANSEN, Keith	970
16	HANSEN, Cindy	
17	SEPAROVICH Shelley	980
18	FREDEEN, Mary	990
19	WEST, Barbara	
20	WEST, Barbara	1000
21	D'ANDREA, Chris	1010

SOUTH BEACH ANNEX		
Lot#	Name	St#
1A	HANSON, Steve	
1	HANSON, Rebecca	1220
2	HANSON, Steve	
3	HEMPLER, Portia	1210
4	GALLAGHER, Rosalynn	
5	GALLAGHER, Neil	1200
6	MILLIKAN, Michael	
7	CLINE, Shane	
8	ANKENY, Dennis	1190
9	ANKENY, D.	
10	JINKS, Carol	1180
11	PORTH, Don	1170
12	ERICKSON, Karl	1160
13	GAUTHIER, Melanie	
14	KVINSLAND, Lonny	1150
15	KENNEDY, Debbie	
16	MEYER, Chris	1140
17	VAN DIVER, Marianne	1130
18	LEE, B.	
19	LEE, Betsy	
20	LEE, B.	1120
21	BROOKS, Michelle	1110
22	MCQUEEN, Clyde	1100
23	MCQUEEN, Colleen	
24	KENNEDY, John	
25	KENNEDY, Jan	1090
26	EDWARDS, Ed	1080
27	EDWARDS, Rosemarie	
28	HAWLEY, Mark	1070
29	GEMMILL, Vanessa	1064
30	HOLMES, Diane	1060
31	MONROE, Yvonne	1050
32	SHORT, Ruth	1040
33	BUMGARNER, Jim	
34	BUMGARNER, Susan	1030
35	O'LEARY, Keith	
36	CLUB PROPERTY	
37	HENRY, Ron	1020
38	HENRY, Susan	
39	FREELOVE, J.D.	
40	FREELOVE, J.D.	
41	D'ANDREA, Chris	

BECKETT POINT FISHERMENS CLUB
163 LEASEHOLD LOTS - Leaseholders of Record 06/30/19

BECKETT POINT FISHERMENS CLUB ASSESSORS PLAT RECORDED 06/24/08 #535120

Leasehold - a property held by a Lease

Ground Lease - agreement permitting use of a specific Lot

* **Lot #** - Your leased lot (left column)
* **ST #** - Street Number (right column)

HILL PARK

Lot#	Name	St#
5A	WEISSMANN, Katherine	
4A	MOSES, Chuck	644
3A	MOSES, Lila	
2A	DISHINGTON, Robert	642
1A	ACREE, Kathy	
1	ACREE, Kathy	
2	ACREE, Kathy	554
3	ELAN, Zachary	552
4	ELAN, Zachary	
5	KORINEK, Michael	556
6	HEYCKE, Christine	
7	KORINEK, Michael	
8	CLEMENTS, Mahlon	494
9	CLEMENTS, Mahlon	
10	MOGA, Greg	492
11	MOGA, Greg	
12	MOGA, Greg	
13	MOGA, Greg	
14	MOGA, Greg	

HIGHWAY HEIGHTS

Lot#	Name	St#
1	MURPHY, Patrick	501
1A	HUDSON, Tracy	
2A	CAMFIELD, Kevin	495
3A	CAMFIELD, Heidi	
4A	CLUB PROPERTY	
5A	CLUB PROPERTY	
6	SANDER Trust	
7	SANDER Trust	553
8	KINNEY, Peter	555
9	KINNEY, Peter	
10	MILLAR, Janet	557
11	MILLAR, Janet	
12	MILLAR, Janet	
13	SANDBERG, Nancy	
14	SANDBERG, Nancy	559
15	SANDBERG, Nancy	
16	CLUB PROPERTY	

OLYMPIC VIEW

Lot#	Name	St#
1	CHAN, Arnold	578
2	CHAN, Diana	
3	CHAN, Arnold	576
4	CHAN, Diana	
5	SUDOL, Robert	574
6	JONES, Diane	572
7	CLUB PROPERTY	
8	CLUB PROPERTY	

NORTH BEACH

Lot #	Name	St#
1	AVERILL, Julie	
2	BOLAM, Cindy	10
3	LOGUE, Rev. Gary	20
4	YOUNG, Charles	30
5	LANG, Alec	40
6	MYERS, Carolyn	50
7	POWERS, Randy	60
8	FOUTS, Deb	70
8A	WHITE, Ann	80
9	GUPTILL, Joy	90
10	SCHMUCKER, Larry	100
11	DEBERANARDI, K.	110
12	MYERS, David	120
13	CARL, Randy	130
14	ENGLUND, John	
15	ENGLUND, K.	140
16	NELSON, Leigh	150
17	NELSON, Leigh	
18	BEHAR, Dana	160

WEST BEACH

Lot#	Name	St#
1	DEROUSIE, Mike	850
2	LUX, Diane	840
3	FINNIGAN, Eileen	834
4	O'DELL, Lynn	830
5	CAMPBELL, Larry	
6	CAMPBELL, Kathy	820
7	ERICKSON, Aleta	
8	BURKE, Gene	810
9	WALLIN, Janet	800
10	CAMBURN, Tom	790
11	ROSS, Connie	780
12	ROSS, Darren	
13	RANSOM, Sean	760
14	RANSOM, Sean	
15	JOHNSON, Katherine	750
16	CAMFIELD, Heidi	740
17	CAMFIELD, Kevin	
18	SCHICK, Linda	730
19	CARR, Margaret	720
20	CARR, Margaret	
21	HAWKINS, Jerry	710
22	BRANTLEY, Angela	
23	BRANTLEY, Angela	700
24	AURDAL, Nanette	690
25	AURDAL, Steve	
26	AURDAL, Nanette	680
27	AURDAL, Steve	
28	OFFIELD, Wendy	670
29	OFFIELD, Wendy	
30	ALBERTSON, Tina	660
31	OLSEN, Lorraine	
32	OLSEN, Lorraine	650
33	EASTER, Cy	
34	EASTER, Cy	640
35	ANDERSON, Jon	630
36	DARLING, Pamela	
37	DARLING, Pamela	610

NOTES, RESEARCH AND SOURCES

The club logo used prior to 1995 depicts the chart drawn by H.M.S. Discovery of Discovery Bay and published in charting the Northwest Coast. The logo used since depicts Discovery Bay with the Olympics as the background.

In my research through some 70 years of club records the pattern of member participation in club affairs was clear. Without the extraordinary efforts of the membership the community would not exist as it does today. In very few instances were projects completely done by outside contractors, nearly always being accomplished and overseen by club committees and membership. While names of the more active members changed with the projects and the decades, the underlying organizers efforts always seemed to remain. The secretaries for the most part have held long periods of office and have been the most instrumental in overseeing club projects and dealing with the day to day concerns of some 160 members.

SECRETARIES:

Patti Sahlinger	1998 - present
Margaret Maurice	1996 – 1997
Carol Keogh	1990 – 1996
Marge Cipriotti	1983 – 1990
Diane Lux	1975 – 1983
Jean Morello	1973 – 1975
Mae Cook	1963 – 1973
Charles Seeley	1950 – 1962
E. W. Drake	1940 – 1950

It has been an interesting and challenging project going through the records for the past 70 years of Beckett Point's development.

Neil Gallagher

SOURCES

1) Vancouver's Voyage – *Charting the Northwest Coast*, Robin Fisher – Pages 24, 25, 27, 29

2) History of Protection Island – Jefferson County Historical Society

3) History of Jefferson County and Discovery Bay - Jefferson County Historical Society

4) Beckett Point record files

5) Becket Point Club publications

6) Port Townsend Leader

7) Web site: Beckett Point.com

8) Input by club members

Made in the USA
Middletown, DE
13 August 2019